I0019595

SQL

Simplified SQL Programming & Database Management For Beginners. Your Step-By-Step Guide to Learning The SQL Database.

Steve Gosling

Table of Contents

© Copyright 2018 - All rights reserved.

It is not legal to reproduce, duplicate, or transmit any part of this document in either electronic means or in printed format. Recording of this publication is strictly prohibited.

Introduction

Congratulations for purchasing and downloading this eBook on simplified SQL programming and managing databases for beginners. You have made a wise decision on investing in this material that will provide you all the necessary fundamental skills in starting your career as a database programmer. It is true that there a lot of resources out there, but the challenge is finding the right one that is easy for you to understand in a fun way. Here, you will learn the best methods of how to extract and manipulate data using SQL - a powerful database management tool. In addition, this eBook will make you realize that there are boundless SQL career opportunities that are in store for you.

I am Steve and I have experienced first-hand how SQL have become an integral part in extracting, creating, manipulating and analyzing database information. Thus, I would like to share with you the knowledge that I have gained as I explored the world of database management and SQL programming. I assure you that this eBook will present you the essential tool kit to understand the software language in a fun and easy way. As you go along with the best practices that I have presented here, you will be able to confidently start your profession as an SQL database scientist.

I can promise that with this book you will be able to comprehend what you thought was hard to accomplish in SQL. You will be educated on how and why this amazing programming language came into existence, the step-by-step software installation process, the programming environment suitable for the beginner level, and some supplementary advanced topics. These are simply what you need to unleash your talents and skills in becoming an SQL database professional, eventually securing you a potentially high paying occupation in the future.

Embark on your journey now in exploring the SQL programming language and managing databases. Let this eBook serve as your ultimate guide in learning the various technical skills and fully appreciating the amazing wonders of this programming language in a cool way! So, what are you waiting for? Don't waste any more time and let's get started!

Chapter One: SQL Overview

In this chapter you will learn an overview of the SQL history, why and how it came to existence. Understanding the background of this computer language will help you realize its importance to most IT professionals who decided to focus on gaining expertise in the field of data management. Such knowledge will further guide you in maximizing the potentials of the SQL language as a programming tool.

Investing in technology that will efficiently and effectively gather, analyze, manipulate and present raw data into meaningful information is the main priority of almost all businesses today - from small to large scale enterprises. A powerful data management technology will surely give a company the expertise it needs to stay competitive or even ahead of its competitors. That is why Structured Query Language, or more popularly known as SQL (pronounced as "ess-que-el" or "see'qwl"), has been formulated as a standard tool for database administrators, developers or analysts to communicate with databases.

SQL History

An American multinational technology and consulting company called International Business Machines Corporation, or simply IBM, initiated the invention of a computer database language in the 1970s. Their prototype design was based on the scientific paper written by Dr. E. F. Codd entitled *"A Relational Model of Data for Large Shared Data Banks"* and was originally called SEQUEL (Structured English QUEry Language). The primary function of the program was to collect, organize and process databases. Enhancement features were included to the computer software to improve its performance, such as implementing and managing database security. It was eventually renamed to SQL, which stands for Structured Query Language, when IBM researchers found out that the same "Sequel" trademark was being used by another company.

SQL had already gone through many versions since it was first released to the public. Each database software type or version can be identified using the developer that created the said program. In 1979, Oracle Corporation, which was formerly known as Relational Software, Incorporated, released the first SQL product called ORACLE. With the increasing demand for data management applications, SQL has turned into an industry standard in the field of Information Technology (IT). This formal standard was further maintained by the International Standards Organization, or simply known as ISO. SQL, as implemented by IBM, was established as the database communication benchmark in 1986. Another organization named American National Standards Institute (ANSI), which authorizes certain standards in numerous US industries, developed another database application called ANSI SQL. This was eventually adopted by ISO as one of the international standards in 1987. Further revisions of the standards have followed, such as SQL-92 and SQL-99, that were released in 1992 and 1999 respectively. The latest one is now called SQL-2011 that was officially launched in December 2011. To conclude, ANSI and ISO are the two international committees that guard and maintain various SQL standards.

SQL Features

Just like what was previously mentioned, SQL is an ISO and ANSI standard database computer language that allows users to create, update, delete, retrieve and present data in a meaningful way. One can easily understand and learn the commands used in this program, which were patterned using the English language. Commonly used SQL statements are select, add, update, insert, delete, create and alter. Because of the program's simple-ness, managing databases is less complicated, without having to write complex codes. In addition, SQL is a comprehensive utility that can be used to efficiently and quickly retrieve large amounts of information from a database for analysis.

Below are some of the factors why SQL has transformed to become the standard computer database management tool in almost any type of platform:

Computer system portability - SQL can run in mainframes, personal computers (PCs), laptops and even hand-held devices, such as mobile phones, with or without internet connectivity. This also means that you can transfer databases from one device to another without facing any problems.

Easy to understand statements/commands - SQL structure is characterized as a declarative language, which mainly consists of English statements, so that a novice user could easily start programming in no time.

Interactive programming environment - SQL can be used immediately to interact with databases and quickly process complex instructions.

Multiple data views - SQL provides multiple views of database content and structure to different users.

Dynamic database access and definition with internet connectivity - SQL enables dynamic changes to the database structure within a three-tiered Internet architecture (client, application server and a database), even if such database is being accessed by different users at one time.

Complete database language - SQL contains all the commands and functions required to manipulate databases.

Java integration - SQL has been designed to integrate with Java through an application programming interface (API) called Java Database Connectivity (JDBC).

SQL Applications

Generally, you have to pay for the database application programs when you download them. However, there are some open sourced SQL versions that are free to use where the original program can be modified by anyone. Still, these numerous versions are not exactly the same and a database program or server is required to access and manipulate the data. With this, most software vendors have developed their own servers for such database applications. Below is a table of some of the major vendors and their servers.

VENDOR NAME	SERVERS
Oracle	Oracle Database SQL
IBM	DB2
Microsoft	SQL Server
Other Open Source	MySQL, PostgreSQL

With the current shift from merely producing products and providing services, the corporate world is discovering innovative ways on how to invest in powerful SQL database applications that are capable of handling vast amounts of data. The primary objective is transforming raw data to meaningful pieces of information that will lead to improving company processes. Such enhancements on data manipulation will further generate more profitable business insights. One might also think that only computer professionals, like database administrators and developers, will benefit from using this all-powerful tool. Take note that knowing at least a little about SQL could be an advantage for people in various roles, from a simple data encoder to a database scientist. SQL is not only applicable for programming geeks because its semantics can enable a non-IT personnel to understand data flow and manipulation that drives every company. Moreover, stepping up your computer programming skills using this language opens several career opportunities, whether in the managerial, analytical, research or IT fields.

Chapter Summary

- Different software vendors have developed their own versions of SQL since it was first released to the public in the 1970s.
- SQL follows the ANSI and ISO database programming standards.
- Numerous factors are taken into consideration in transforming SQL as the standard computer database management tool.
- Understanding SQL semantics will give you a leverage in improving business processes and further take your professional career to the next level.

In the next chapter you will learn the fundamentals of the SQL environment that include the database structure, program's essential components and step-by-step software installation.

Chapter Two: SQL Environment Fundamentals

In this chapter you will learn the fundamental database structure and characteristics of the SQL software environment. Gaining such understanding will make you realize why the business world now is geared to retrieve and manipulate data to bring forth a more profitable income.

Database Structure

Before learning the technical aspects of SQL as a programming language, you need to understand first what a database is and its elements. There are numerous ways of defining and describing a database, but basically it is a collection of items existing for a certain period of time. Just imagine a calling card holder as a database that organizes all your business cards containing various information of different people (example: complete name, job title, company name and contact details), who you may or may not know personally. A more professional definition is that a database is an organized tool capable of keeping data or information related to one another, which can be efficiently and effectively retrieved when the need arises.

When such conceptual information is being represented digitally or physically, then a *record* is created. From the previous calling card holder example, if you want to keep track of your business contacts then each business card will be assigned to a specific record that contains several pieces of information for a particular contact person. These pieces of information are now called the record's *attributes*. Another element is the *metadata*, which contains the information that defines or describes the structure of the data contained in the database. All this information will then be stored in only one region called the *data dictionary* to enhance data retrieval and organization.

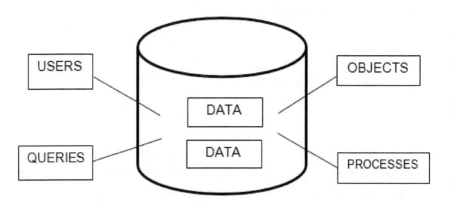

The illustration above shows how the database elements are integrated to one another. The database contains the data needed by the various users of an organization. From these sets of data, different *objects* are created, such as tables and views that present information in a more readable way. Next, are the *queries* or inquiries into the database that will extract data and present it according to the user's requirements. Lastly, we have the database processes that will handle other user requests.

Databases are also categorized into three types, depending on the size, the machinery in which it runs and how big the organization that manages it is:

- **Personal Database** – Cconceptualized and designed by a single person, this database is implemented on stand-alone computers. Its structure is simple, and the size is relatively small. An example is your electronic personal address book.

- **Workgroup/Departmental Database** – Developed by individuals of a particular workgroup or department within an organization, this database is larger and more complex as compared to the personal type. This can also be accessed by multiple users at the same time.

- **Enterprise Database** – This type of database is capable of handling the entire flow of a massive system of information required by very large organizations. Thus, its design involves far more complex structures.

SQL Program Components

Before you start coding in SQL, it is a must that you understand its programming components first. These components include the basic commands used in performing various database functions.

Data Definition Language (DDL)

This SQL language component enables the user to create, change or restructure, and even destroy elements or objects when they are not needed in the database. DDL focuses only on the structure and not the data contained within the elements. The main DDL commands are:

o   **CREATE** – This command is responsible for building database structures like tables and views.

o   **DROP** – This command is the reverse of the CREATE statement that destroys the database structure by removing them from the database.

o   **ALTER** – This command changes the database structure by adding or removing columns from a table or view in the database.

Data Manipulation Language (DML)

This component consists of SQL commands that handle data manipulation and maintenance functions. This means that the user is able to select, enter, change or remove data within the table. These are the four main DML commands:

o   **SELECT** – This command selects rows of data from a certain table.

o   **INSERT** – This command inserts new data values or rows of data into a certain table.

o   **UPDATE** – This command modifies or alters pre-existing data values or rows of data in a table. One table or multiple rows/columns of a particular table are updated within a database.

o   **DELETE** – This command is used to remove certain records or rows of data from the table (or even the entire table itself).

Data Control Language (DCL)

This SQL component consists of commands that allow the user to manage data access within the database through user privileges. Also, accidental or intentional misuse of information by database

17

users are prevented. All SQL statements that perform any database operation are captured and saved in a log file. These are the main DCL command:

o   **GRANT** – This command provides a user with certain privileges by giving him the permission to access the database.

o   **REVOKE** – This command removes a user's privileges or permission to access the database.

Now that you have become familiar with the common SQL commands, the next step is how to install the software language successfully into your PC or laptop. First, before setting up what SQL version is applicable for your device, you must determine the purpose, *why* you need to have a database. This will further identify other database design requirements such as size, type of machine where the application will run, storage medium, complexity and more. When you start figuring out such database requirements, you also need to know up to what level of specifications should be taken into consideration in your design. Having too much design details will result in a very complex database that might only waste time and effort, and especially the storage space of your device. On the other hand, insufficient detail specifications will lead to a poor performing and inefficient database. Once you have finalized the database design phase, then you can decide which programming software you can download to begin your SQL experience journey.

SQLite Installation

For this eBook's discussion, you will have gain first-hand know-how on using SQLite. This a simple software library that is recommended as a database engine starter for someone who is at a beginner level to design, build and deploy applications. Developed by Richard Hipp and his team of programmers, SQLite is a free and stand-alone database software that is quick to download and easy to administer. It can be easily configured and implemented and does not require any client-server setup at all. Because of this accessibility and flexibility, SQLite has been regarded as one of the most widely used free database software applications worldwide.

These are some of the distinct features of the SQLite database programming language:

- **Server-less with zero configuration** - SQLite does not require any special setup procedure in configuring files nor a separate server process.

- **Easy compilation with a readable source code** - SQLite source code was designed to be simple and accessible, even for an average user.

- **Compact** - SQLite library is no more than 500KiB in size and its code footprint is significantly small. Also, any unnecessary features are disabled at compile-time to further reduce the library size.

- **Stable Cross-Platform Database Portability** - SQLite file format written on one device can be used on another machine with a different architecture or platform. It was also designed to be stable and compatible, at all times, where newer versions of SQLite can read and write older database files.

To install the database software, you need to go to the application's download page of the SQLite website.

1. Go to https://www.sqlite.org/.

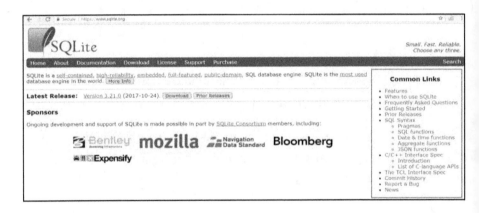

2. Click the *Download* menu on top, just below the SQLite logo. This will take you to the page where you would choose and download the appropriate version of SQLite for your device platform (e.g., Windows, Mac or Linux).

3. For this e-Book's discussion, choose the 64-bit Windows platform. Go to the *Pre-Compiled Binaries for Windows* section and click on *sqlite-dll-win64-x64-3210000.zip* and *sqlite-tools-win32-x86-3210000.zip* to download all the necessary command-line tools for manipulating database files in SQLite.

4. Create a new folder named *C:\SQLite* where you will be extracting all the content of the files that was downloaded previously.

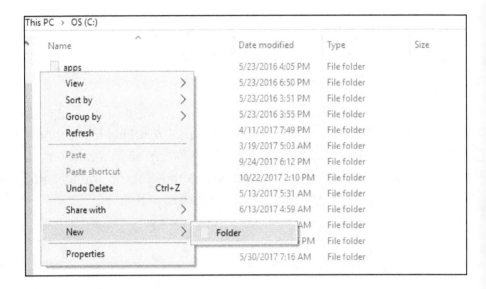

5. Go to the *Downloads* folder in your computer and find the two zip files shown below:

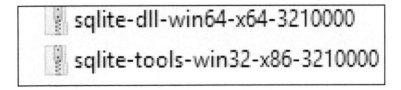

6.   Double-click on the zip file named *sqlite-dll-win64-x64-3210000.zip* and click on the *Extract all* button. Set the destination folder to *C:\SQLite* and then click *Extract*.

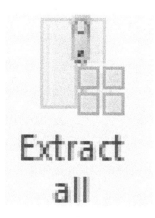

As for the *sqlite-tools-win32-x86-3210000.zip*, double-click this zip file then open the *sqlite-tools-win32-x86-3210000* subfolder. Extract all the files to the same *C:\SQLite* folder.

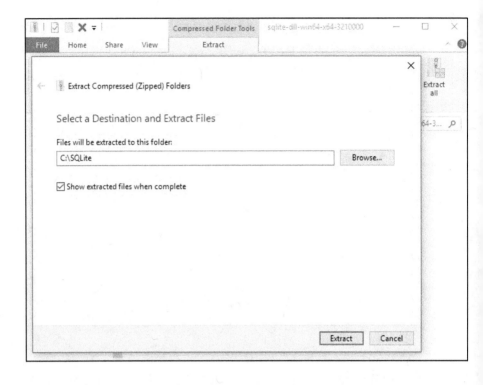

You should now have the following files inside *C:\SQLite* folder:

To verify the installation and use the SQLite program, you have to execute it using the command line window by performing the following steps:

1. Launch the command line from your Windows menu.

2.   You will now have the black *Command Prompt* window on your computer/laptop screen.

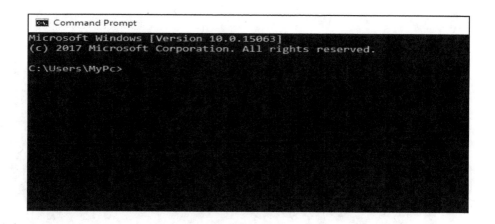

3.   Type *cd c:\sqlite* and press enter to navigate to the folder where the SQL files are located.

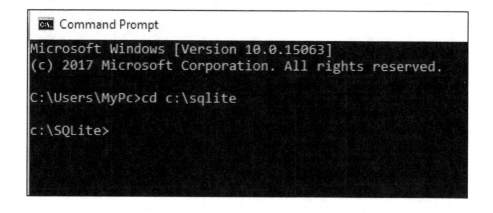

4.   Enter *sqlite3* to execute the program. You can also type *.help* to view all the available commands in SQLlite3.

```
Command Prompt - sqlite3
C:\Users\MyPc>cd c:\sqlite

c:\SQLite>sqlite3
SQLite version 3.21.0 2017-10-24 18:55:49
Enter ".help" for usage hints.
Connected to a transient in-memory database.
Use ".open FILENAME" to reopen on a persistent database.
sqlite> .help
.auth ON|OFF            Show authorizer callbacks
.backup ?DB? FILE      Backup DB (default "main") to FILE
.bail on|off           Stop after hitting an error.  Default OFF
.binary on|off         Turn binary output on or off.  Default OFF
.cd DIRECTORY          Change the working directory to DIRECTORY
.changes on|off        Show number of rows changed by SQL
.check GLOB            Fail if output since .testcase does not match
.clone NEWDB           Clone data into NEWDB from the existing database
.databases             List names and files of attached databases
.dbinfo ?DB?           Show status information about the database
.dump ?TABLE? ...      Dump the database in an SQL text format
                         If TABLE specified, only dump tables matching
                         LIKE pattern TABLE.
.echo on|off           Turn command echo on or off
.eqp on|off|full       Enable or disable automatic EXPLAIN QUERY PLAN
.exit                  Exit this program
.fullschema ?--indent? Show schema and the content of sqlite_stat tables
.headers on|off        Turn display of headers on or off
.help                  Show this message
.import FILE TABLE     Import data from FILE into TABLE
.imposter INDEX TABLE  Create imposter table TABLE on index INDEX
```

The screen above may not seem to be very user-friendly. So, if you want to work with your databases using an intuitive yet fast and powerful graphical user interface (GUI) tool, you need to download *SQLiteStudio*. This is a free and portable database manager and editor. All you need to do is download, unpack and run the application. Follow these simple steps in downloading SQLiteStudio in Windows 10:

1. Go to https://sqlitestudio.pl/index.rvt and click on the *Download* menu between *Gallery* and *Changelog* menus.

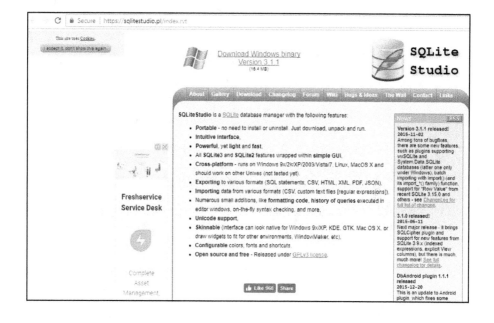

2. Click the appropriate link that matches the version of your computer's operating system to start the software download.

Lastest stable release (3.1.1):

Distribution	Platform	Size	Version	Link
Windows	32-bit	16.4MB	3.1.1	sqlitestudio-3.1.1.zip
Linux	64-bit	18.7MB	3.1.1	sqlitestudio-3.1.1.tar.xz
MacOSX	64-bit (ix86_64)	25.2MB	3.1.1	sqlitestudio-3.1.1.dmg
Sources (zip)	Independent	9.0MB	3.1.1	sqlitestudio-3.1.1.zip
Sources (tar.gz)	Independent	8.3MB	3.1.1	sqlitestudio-3.1.1.tar.gz

..::All files - click here::..

..::Old, unsupported versions (2.x.x) - click here::..

3.   After downloading the file, extract all of its the contents to the same *C:\SQLite* folder. You will now have *SQLiteStudio* subfolder.

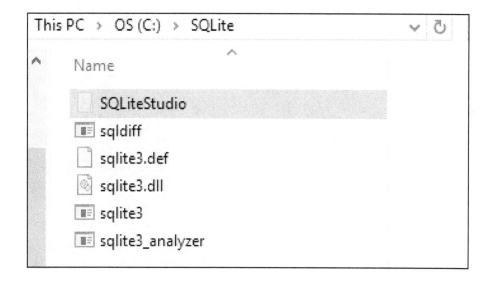

4. If you want to create an SQLiteStudio shortcut on your desktop so you can quickly launch the application, open the *SQLiteStudio* subfolder in the *SQLite* folder. Right-click on the *SQLiteStudio* filename, select *Send to* option then choose *Desktop (create shortcut)*.

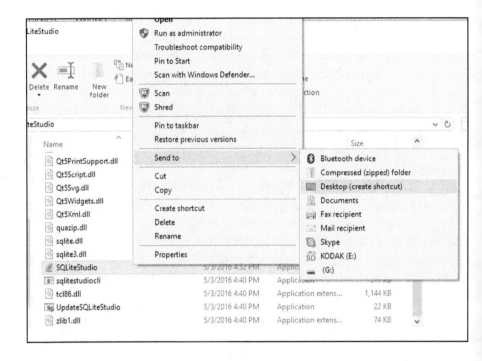

5.   You will now have the *SQLiteStudio* icon on your desktop. To launch the database application, double-click the icon to get the following screen:

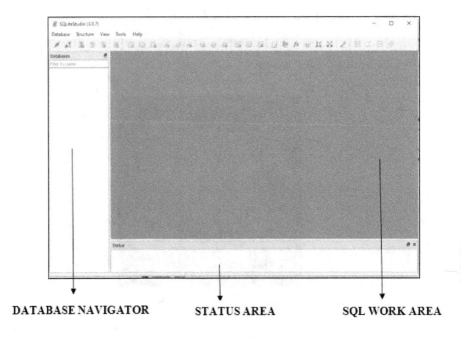

DATABASE NAVIGATOR   **STATUS AREA**   **SQL WORK AREA**

The white space at the left is the *Database Navigator* that displays all the database elements like tables and views. The big grey space at the middle is the *SQL Work Area*, where all the programming statements or commands will be written. Lastly, the space at the bottom is the *Status Area* where execution program messages are indicated if needed.

Chapter Summary

- A database is a digital tool that organizes and keeps data/information, which can be retrieved effectively and efficiently upon the request of the user.
- A database consists of elements (e.g., objects, queries, processes and more) and can be categorized into three types - personal, workgroup/departmental and enterprise.
- The SQL program component consists of the following basic commands - data definition language (DDL), data manipulation language (DML) and data control language (DCL)
- SQLite is a free and stand-alone database software developed by Richard Hipp that you can execute via the command prompt or its GUI tool (SQLite Studio).

In the next chapter you will learn what data objects in SQL are and their importance. You will also have an in-depth knowledge about database schemas and tables.

Chapter Three: Database Objects

In this chapter you will learn what database objects are, their importance and how they relate to one another. You will also know how to manipulate some of the common SQL database objects like schemas and tables.

Defining a Database Object

To begin with, *objects* are the logical units that make up the building blocks of a database, which store or reference to a particular data. They represent the information that you consider to be the important aspects of your database model. That is why defining these objects is the first step in database design. There are objects that should be considered as major entities that are essential in generating results to user requests, while others serve as supplemental to those major ones. You might even realize that some of these objects should not be included in the model at all.

Defining a Schema

When database objects are collected together and then connected to one particular database, it becomes a *schema*. There could be one or multiple schemas related to a given database. A user turns into a *schema owner*, when he associates himself with that group of objects or even when he creates his own objects. In addition, a schema owner has total control over these objects that he has created, manipulated or deleted. For example, you were assigned *DBUSER1* as your username to access the system by the database administrator. Once you log on to the database and start creating a table called *EMPLOYEE_TBL1*, the actual name of this table is *DBUSER1.EMPLOYEE_TBL1* and the schema name is *USER1*.

Defining a Table

Let us take the discussion further into a more technical aspect. When database elements are integrated to one another, they create relationships among objects. Thus, the entity becomes a *relational database*. This database model was formulated in 1970 by Dr. E. F. Codd. According to him, database performance could be optimized if you simplify data into smaller yet more logical units of information.

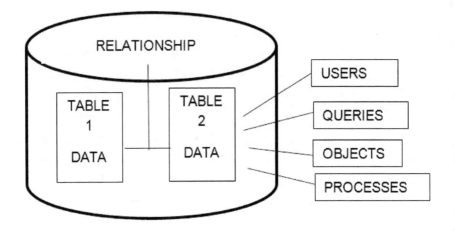

In this illustration (which is similar to the previous one), you will notice the two sets of data are now presented as tables that are connected to each other using relationships. As the primary storage of data, a table consists of rows and columns, which keeps the data needed by the user. In a relational database, tables should be related to one another to improve the data retrieval process. Try to picture out a Microsoft Excel spreadsheet that contains information from your calling card holder. Assume that these are your clients that have ordered products and services from your company. You will then have a CUSTOMER TABLE, that may look similar to the following:

CUSTOMER ID	NAME	POSITION	COMPANY	STATE	CONTACT NO
1	Kathy Ale	President	Tile Industrial	TX	3461234567
2	Kevin Lord	VP	Best Tooling	NY	5181234567
3	Kim Ash	Director	Car World	CA	5101234567
4	Abby Karr	Manager	West Mart	NV	7751234567

To store the information about the orders that your customers have made (order ID, date, quantity and more), you will need the ORDER TABLE below:

ORDER ID	ORDER DATE	CUSTOMER ID	PRODUCT ID	ORDER QTY
1	2016-05-23	1	4	300
2	2016-09-09	1	5	100
3	2016-02-17	3	2	150
4	2016-05-12	2	2	500

Going back to the CUSTOMER TABLE, a row is also known as a customer's *record* or a *tuple* that stores information for every single customer. Meanwhile, a column or *field* contains a single *attribute* or a specific type of information about the customer, such as his name, job title or position, company name and address, and contact number. For each column, it will contain the same type of data in every row. So, if a column should store the names of your customer, then its corresponding rows will have to contain all your customers' names. Analyzing the two tables further, you will notice that both of them have a column that contains the same data – *CUSTOMER ID*. This data value is what we call the *common key* that shows the relationship between the *CUSTOMER TABLE* and the *ORDER TABLE,* linking them together within a relational database. It is through these common keys that the merging of data from multiple tables is possible to form a larger set of entity.

To demonstrate the relationship between the two tables further, we will create a two-dimensional array of data by combining two attributes (CUSTOMER ID and CUSTOMER NAME) that corresponds to the given ORDER ID:

ORDER ID	CUSTOMER ID	CUSTOMER NAME
1	1	Kathy Ale
2	1	Kathy Ale
3	3	Kim Ash
4	2	Kevin Lord

A *cell* is a particular section in the table where a row and a column intersect. Every cell should only contain single-valued entries and no two rows are the exactly same - meaning each cell has only one value and there will be no duplicate rows. In the table above, you can see that there is no empty cell and no two customers have the same *ORDER ID*.

Chapter Summary

- Objects are the building blocks of a database model and defining them is the very first step in database design.
- A schema shows how objects are collected together and how these elements are connected to the database.
- Dr. E. F. Codd formulated the relational database in 1970 that shows how database elements are interrelated to one another.
- A table is the primary storage of data that consists of rows (records or tuples) and columns (fields that contain attributes). A cell is the intersection of a row and a column.

In the next chapter you will learn what a data type is and its significance to the database design. You will also gain understanding on the characteristics of the general SQL data types and their available subtypes.

Chapter Four: SQL Data Types

In this chapter you will learn the role of data in a database model, how it is defined, its characteristics and the various types that the SQL software supports. There are general data types that are further categorized into different subtypes. It is advisable that you use defined data types to ensure the portability and comprehensibility of the database model.

Data Definition

Data is the stored information in a database that you can manipulate anytime that you want. If you can remember the calling card example in Chapter 3, its database model is a collection of customers' names, contact numbers, company addresses, job titles and so on. When rules are provided on how to write and store data, then you need to have a clear understanding of the different *data types*. You need to take into consideration the length or space allocated by the database for every table column and what data values it should contain - whether it is just all letters or all numbers, combination or alphanumeric, graphical, date or time. By defining what data type is stored in each field during the design phase, data entry errors will be prevented. This is the *field definition* process, a form of validation that controls how incorrect data is to be entered into the database.

When a certain database field does not have any data items at all, then the value is unknown or what is called a *null value*. This is completely different from the numeric zero or the blank character value, since zeroes and blanks are still considered definite values. Check out the following scenarios when you might have a null value:

- Even if the data value could possibly exist, you don't know what it is yet.
- The value does not really exist yet.
- The value could be out of range.
- The field is not appropriate for a particular row.

SQL Data Types

These are the general types of SQL data types and their subtypes.

- **Numeric** – The value defined by this data type is either an exact or an approximate number.

o **Exact Numeric**

▪ **INTEGER** – This consists of positive and negative whole numbers without any decimal nor a fractional part. The INTEGER data value ranges from negative 2,147,483,648 to positive 2,147,483,647, with a maximum storage size of four bytes.

- **SMALLINT** – This replaces integers when you want to save some storage space. However, its precision cannot be larger than that of an integer. Precision in computer programming is the maximum total of significant digits a certain number can have. The SMALLINT data value ranges from negative 32,768 to positive 32,767, with a maximum storage size of two bytes.

- **BIGINT** – This is the reverse of SMALLINT, in which the minimum precision is the same or greater than that of an INTEGER. The BIGINT data value ranges from negative 9,223,372,036,854,775,808 to positive 9,223,372,036,854,775,807, with a maximum storage size of eight bytes.

- **NUMERIC (p, s)** – This data type contains an integer part and a fractional part that indicates the precision and scale of the data value. Scale is the number of digits reserved in the fractional part of the data value (located at the right side of the decimal point). In NUMERIC (p, s), *'p'* specifies the precision while *'s'* specifies the scale. For example, NUMERIC (6, 3) means that the number has a total of 6 significant digits with 3 digits following the decimal point. Therefore, its absolute value will only be up to 999.999.

- **DECIMAL (p, s)** – This also has a fractional component where you can specify both the data value's precision and scale, but allows for greater precision. For example, DECIMAL (6, 3)

44

can contain values up to 999.999 but the database will still accept values larger than 999.999 by rounding off the number. Let us say you entered the number 123.4564, the value that will be stored is 123.456. Thus, the precision given specifies the allocated storage size for this data type.

    o   **Approximate Numeric**

- **REAL (s)** – This is a single-precision, floating-point number where the decimal point can "float" within the said number. This gives a limitless precision and a scale of variable lengths for the data type's decimal value. For example, the values for π (pi) can include 3.1, 3.14 and 3.14159 (each value has its own precision). This data type's precision ranges from 1 up to 21, with a maximum storage size of four bytes.

- **DOUBLE PRECISION (p, s)** – As what the name suggests, this is a double-precision, floating-point number with a storage capacity of twice the REAL data type. This data type is suitable when you require more precise numbers, such as in most scientific field of disciplines. This data type's precision ranges from 22 up to 53 digits, with a maximum storage size of eight bytes.

- **FLOAT (p, s)** – This data type lets you specify the value's precision and the computer decides whether it will be a single or a double-precision number. It will allow both the precision of REAL and DOUBLE PRECISION data types. Such

45

features make it easier to move the database from one computer platform to another.

- **String** – Considered as the most commonly used data type, this stores alphanumeric information.

    o **CHARACTER (n)** or **CHAR (n)** – Known as a fixed-length string or a constant character, this data type contains strings that have the same length (represented by *'n'*, which is the maximum number of characters allocated for the defined field). For example, setting the column's data type to CHAR (23) means the maximum length of the data to be stored in that field is 23 characters. If its length is less than 23, then the remaining spaces are filled with blanks by SQL. However, this becomes the downside of using fixed-length strings because storage space is totally wasted. On the other hand, if the length is not specified, then SQL assumes a length of just one character. The CHARACTER data type can have a maximum length of 254 characters.

    o **CHARACTER VARYING (n)** or **VARCHAR (n)** – This data type is for entries that have different lengths, but the remaining spaces will not be filled by spaces. This means that the exact number of characters entered will be stored in the database to avoid space wastage. The maximum length for this data type is 32,672 characters with no default value.

o **CHARACTER LARGE OBJECT (CLOB)** – This was introduced in SQL:1999 where the variable-length data type is used, which contains a Unicode, character-based information. Such data is too big to be stored as a CHARACTER type, just like large documents, and the maximum value is up to 2,147,483,647 characters long.

- **Date and Time** – This data type handles information associated with dates and times.

o **DATE** – This provides a storage space for the date's year, month and day values (in that particular order). The value for the year is expressed in four digits (represented by values ranging from 0001 up to 9999), while the month and day values are both represented by any two digits. The format of this data type is: *'yyyy-mm-dd.'*

o **TIME** – This stores and displays time values using an hour-minute-second format (*"HH:MM:SS"*).

o **DATETIME** – This contains both date and time information displayed using the "YYYY-MM-DD HH:MM:SS" format. The range of this data type is from "1000-01-01 00:00:00" to "9999-12-31 23:59:59".

o **TIMESTAMP** – Similar to the DATETIME data type, this ranges from "1970-01-01 00:00:01" UTC to "2038-01-19 03:14:07" UTC.

- **Boolean** – This data type is used for comparing information and based from the results they can return TRUE, FALSE, or NULL values. If all the conditions for a given query are met, then Boolean value returns TRUE. Otherwise, the value is either FALSE or NULL.

User-Defined Data Type

We will now discuss user-defined data types or simply UDT's. By the name itself, the user defines or specifies the data values based on the existing data types. This allows customization to meet other user requirements and maximize the available storage space. Moreover, programmers enjoy the flexibility they bring in developing database applications. UDT's make it possible when you need to store the same type of data in a column that will also be defined in several tables. The CREATE TYPE statement is used to define UDT's.

For example, if you need to use two different currencies for your database like the US dollar and the UK pound, you can create and define the following UDT's:

CREATE TYPE USDollar AS DECIMAL (9, 2) ;

CREATE TYPE UKPound AS DECIMAL (9, 2) ;

Both data types were created using the predefined DECIMAL type and each has its own particular function and characteristic in the database. Using the sample customer and order information from the previous chapters, we will create the following invoice tables that include the two defined UDTs:

```
CREATE TABLE AmericaInvoice (

        InvoiceID    INTEGER            PRIMARY KEY,
        CustomerID   INTEGER,
        OrderID      INTEGER,
        TotalSaleAmt USDollar,
        ShippingFee  USDollar
        ) ;
```

```
CREATE TABLE UnitedKingdomInvoice (
        InvoiceID      INTEGER                 PRIMARY KEY,
        CustomerID  INTEGER,
        OrderID       INTEGER,
        TotalSaleAmt USDollar,
        ShippingFee  USDollar
        ) ;
```

Chapter Summary

- Data is the stored information in a database that a user can define and manipulate.
- There are different general SQL data types, namely numeric, string, date and time, and Boolean.
- If you want to define more specific data types when designing your database model, you can use the different subtypes under each general SQL data type.
- UDT's or user-defined data types are customized and created by the user based on the existing data types, which gives flexibility in developing various database applications.

In the next chapter you will learn the common SQL commands that are used to create, manipulate and retrieve data from a database, in an efficient and effective way.

Chapter Five: SQL Commands

In this chapter you will learn how to define, manipulate and control databases based on user requirements. An in-depth knowledge will be presented on the common SQL commands (DDL, DML, and DCL) that were already introduced in Chapter 2 and encode them using SQLiteStudio.

Considered as one of the special-purpose languages, SQL was designed specifically for data management. It contains three sets of powerful tools that offer the commands you need in creating, modifying, maintaining and providing security for relational databases.

Data Definition Language (DDL) Statements

Data Definition Language or DDL was described earlier as the set of commands that create, change or destroy basic elements, such as tables and schemas of a relational database. By the way, a table consists of columns and rows, while a schema is composed of tables and views. This is what we call the *containment hierarchy* of a relational database.

Before creating anything, you have to conceptualize your database first. Take note of the following reminders when planning your database design:

- Identify all the tables needed and define the columns they must contain.
- Assign each table a *primary key*, which is the column that turns each row of data value unique to avoid record duplication in a table.
- Create logical links between tables by ensuring that every table defined in your database has at least one column in common with at least another table. This is one of the characteristics of a relational database, where table information is related to one another.

Once your design is sound and complete, you can start transferring it to SQLite using its GUI tool. The DDL statements that will be used in programming in SQLiteStudio are *CREATE*, *ALTER* and *DROP*.

CREATE Statement

The SQL CREATE statement is responsible for constructing essential database structures and objects. You might think that creating tables could be effortless, but you have to take into consideration a number of important factors. Planning table structures carefully before their actual implementation can definitely save you time and effort, avoiding any further database reconfiguration or correction.

The following are some of the factors to take into consideration in the creation of tables:

- Type of data contained in the table
- Table and column names
- Assigned primary key
- Column length
- Columns containing null values

Syntax:

CREATE TABLE *TABLE_NAME*
(datafield1 *DATA_TYPE*   [not null],
    datafield2   *DATA_TYPE* [not null],
    datafield3   *DATA_TYPE* [not null],
    datafield4   *DATA_TYPE* [not null],
    datafield5   *DATA_TYPE* [not null]);

The names of the columns are indicated by *datafield1*, *datafield2*, *datafield3*, *datafield4* and *datafield5* and the field data types (what type of data contained in each column) are written inside the parenthesis, separated by commas. Any information inside the brackets are regarded as optional and this SQL statement finally ends with a semicolon.

Based from the CUSTOMER TABLE introduced in Chapter 3, you will create this new database table using SQLiteStudio. First, let us create your database using the following steps:

1.   Double-click the application icon on your desktop to open SQLiteStudio.

2.   From the *DATABASE* menu on top, select *ADD A DATABASE*.

3.   In the *FILE* input box, type **Sample_DB**, which is the name of the new database, then click OK.

You will now have an object named **Sample_DB (SQLite3)** inside the *Database Navigator* pane.

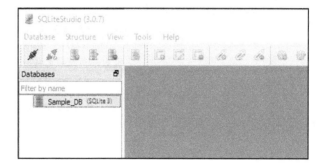

After creating the **Sample_DB** database, we will now create its first table.

1. From the *TOOLS* menu on top (in between *View* and *Help*), select *OPEN SQL EDITOR*. This will launch the SQL editor area at the right pane. Double-clicking **Sample_DB** at the left will show you the *TABLES* and *VIEWS* contained in this database object. Since there are no tables nor views at this time, you will create the CUSTOMER TABLE using the *SQL Editor* pane.

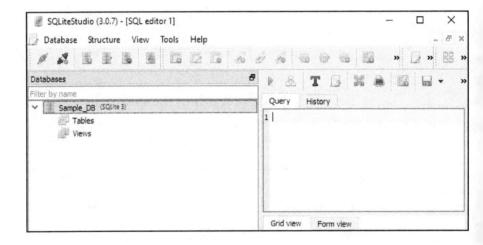

2.   Type the following lines of code under the *QUERY* tab located at the right.

CREATE TABLE Customer_TBL
(CustomerID INTEGER NOT NULL PRIMARY KEY,
CustomerName VARCHAR NOT NULL,
JobPosition VARCHAR,
CompanyName VARCHAR NOT NULL,
USState VARCHAR NOT NULL,
ContactNo BIGINTEGER NOT NULL);


```
Query    History

1 CREATE TABLE Customer_TBL
2 (CustomerID INTEGER NOT NULL PRIMARY KEY,
3     CustomerName VARCHAR NOT NULL,
4     JobPosition VARCHAR,
5     CompanyName VARCHAR NOT NULL,
6     USState VARCHAR NOT NULL,
7     ContactNo BIGINTEGER NOT NULL);|
```

3. To run the lines of code you have entered, click the *EXECUTE QUERY* button ▶ just on top of the *QUERY* tab or simply press F9 on the keyboard. You have now created the **Customer_TBL** table with 6 columns. To check this database object, double-click **Sample_DB** in the *Database Navigator* pane.

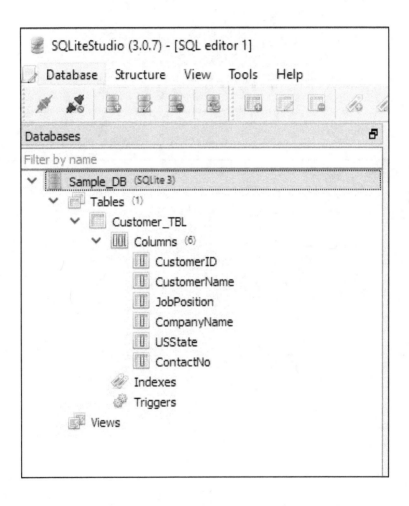

DROP Statement

The SQL DROP statement handles the deletion of existing database objects, such as tables that are not needed anymore. Once the command is performed, all the data and metadata included in the database table are also removed or deleted. Dropping tables is considered to be the simplest command to execute. However, this will cause an error if the table dropped or deleted is being referenced or used by another table in the database model. Thus, the user needs to be very cautious when performing the DROP command statement to avoid removing database objects by mistake, most especially if other users have to access the same database model.

Syntax:

DROP TABLE *TABLE_NAME* [restrict | cascade]

In the syntax statement above, the RESTRICT option returns an error when a table to be dropped is referenced by another table in a given database. The other CASCADE option causes the table and all other referencing database objects to be deleted. However, there are some SQL application programs that do not allow this CASCADE option to ensure that there will be no database objects invalidated.

To drop an existing table, perform the following steps:

1.   If there is only one table existing in the database (**Customer_TBL**), you do not need to use the *RESTRICT* or the *CASCADE* option. Simply enter the line of code below inside the *QUERY* tab.

DROP TABLE Customer_TBL;

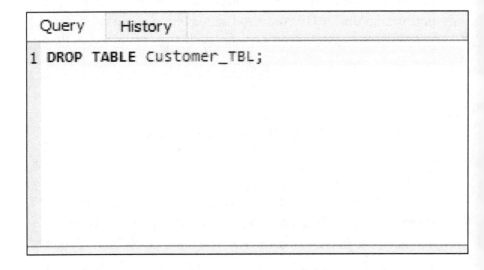

2.   Then click the *EXECUTE QUERY* button and instantaneously the **Customer_TBL** table will be deleted.

ALTER Statement

The SQL ALTER statement is responsible for modifying database objects, specifically tables. Alteration of table elements includes adding and dropping columns, changing the column definitions, adding and dropping constraints, modifying the table's storage values and more.

Syntax:

ALTER TABLE *TABLE_NAME* [modify] [column *COLUMN_NAME*]
[*DATA TYPE* | null not null]
[restrict | cascade]
[drop] [constraint *CONSTRAINT_NAME*]
[add] [column] *COLUMN DEFINITION*;

Follow these steps to alter the **Customer_TBL** table by adding a new column that will contain the company's address of the customer:

1. Type the following lines of code under the *QUERY* tab:

    ```
    ALTER TABLE Customer_TBL ADD
    CompanyAdd VARCHAR;
    ```

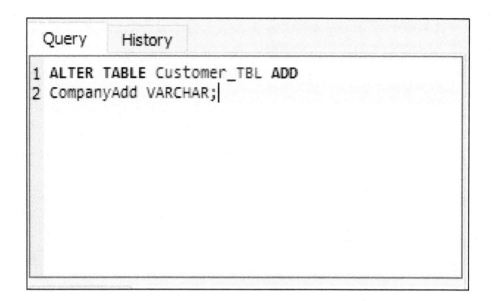

2.   After clicking the *EXECUTE QUERY* button 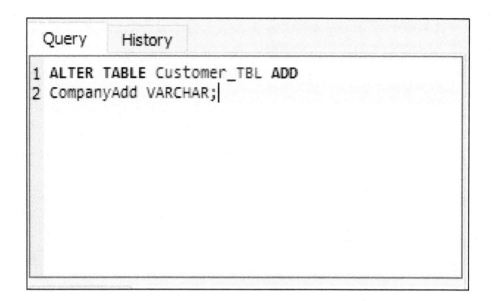 , the **CompanyAdd** column is added after the **ContactNo** column. This field contains values of string data type.

Data Manipulation Language (DML) Statements

Data Manipulation Language (DML) statements are used to manipulate database tables through data selection, insertion, deletion and update. The DML command statements used in the SQLiteStudio are SELECT, INSERT, DELETE and DROP.

Tables are usually empty right after they have been created. The data that can be stored in these objects can be in various formats. Such data format specifications will further determine how the database can be manipulated, which includes selecting data, entering new data, updating existing data and deleting unused data.

SELECT Statement

The most performed manipulation task by database users is retrieving data values. To perform such an operation, you need to use the SELECT command statement in retrieving a single, or multiple records of information from a database table. Retrieving all the records of a particular table is the basic form and most common function of this DML command statement. It is also considered to be the most powerful statement but still it requires other clauses to maximize the function of a query command. The following is the basic SELECT statement syntax:

SELECT * FROM *TABLE_NAME*;

The wildcard character or asterisk sign (*) signifies selecting all the records from a table and listing all the column names of that particular table.

To select all the rows of data from the **Customer_TBL** table:

1.   Click the  option and then type the following:

SELECT * FROM Customer_TBL;

2.   Click the *EXECUTE QUERY* button . The result of the query command is the entire data of the **Customer_TBL** table displayed inside the *GRID VIEW* tab.

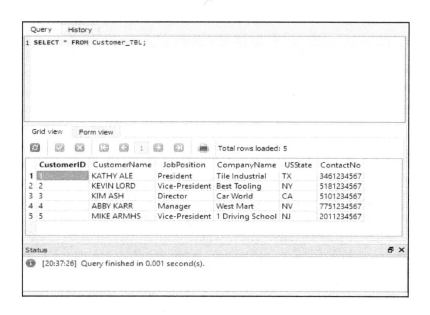

Adding a bit of complexity to the programming lines is required in specifying which rows of data from the database tables are to be retrieved. This is the job of the *WHERE* clause that states a condition and needs to return true for the SELECT operation to be performed. The syntax of this modified SELECT is as follows:

SELECT *COLUMN_LIST*
FROM *TABLE_NAME*
WHERE *CONDITION*;

To select from the **Customer_TBL** table only the rows of data where the customer's job position is "Vice-President":

1.   To go to the *SQL EDITOR*, click the [SQL editor 1] option, then type the following programming lines:

> SELECT *
> FROM Customer_TBL
> WHERE JobPosition = 'Vice-President';

2.   To run the query command, click the *EXECUTE QUERY* button ▶ . Check the results in the *GRID VIEW* tab that displays the records of two customers named Kevin Lord and Mike Armhs (who are both Vice-Presidents of their respective companies).

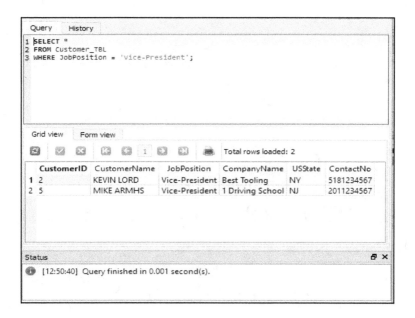

By specifying the columns, you want to retrieve, you are trying to customize your database query results to show what data you really need and how you want them to be displayed. From the previous example, we will modify the programming lines to select only the columns containing the customer's name and company:

1. Change the wildcard character or asterisk sign (*) in the *QUERY* tab into CustomerName and CompanyName by typing the following lines of code:

SELECT CustomerName, CompanyName FROM Customer_TBL WHERE JobPosition = 'Vice-President';

2. To run the command, click the *EXECUTE QUERY* button 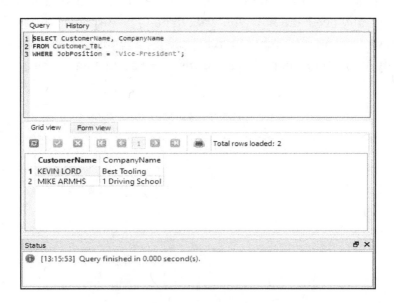. Check the *GRID VIEW* tab to see the results of the query command.

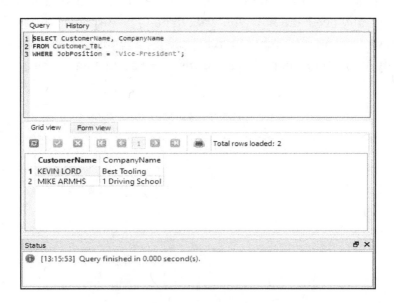

INSERT Statement

Entering new data can be done either manually through individual commands or automatically using a batch of process programs. A number of factors (field length, column data type, table size and more) determine what and how much data can be inserted in your database tables. In populating tables with data, you will use the INSERT statement.

When entering data into a single row of a database table, use the following syntax together with the INSERT statement:

INSERT INTO *TABLE_NAME* [(column_1, column_2, ... , column_n)]
VALUES (value_1, value_2, ..., value_n) ;

Again, anything inside the square brackets are optional and *"n"* indicates the maximum number of columns in the table. The order of the column tables determines the order of the column list. If the items listed inside the VALUES section is in the same order as the table's columns, then the data values will be entered correctly in the corresponding columns. However, indicate the column names if the values are specified in a different order.

Execute the following commands to insert records to the **Customer_TBL** table :

1. In the *SQL EDITOR*, type the following lines :

INSERT INTO Customer_TBL (CustomerID, CustomerName, JobPosition, CompanyName, USState, ContactNo)
VALUES (1, 'Kathy Ale', 'President', 'Tile Industrial', 'TX', 3461234567)

```
Query    History
1 INSERT INTO Customer_TBL (CustomerID, CustomerName, JobPosition, CompanyName, USState, ContactNo)
2 VALUES (1, 'Kathy Ale', 'President', 'Tile Industrial', 'TX', 3461234567)
```

2. Click the *EXECUTE QUERY* button ▶ . If the execution is successful, then there should be no errors in the *Status Area*:

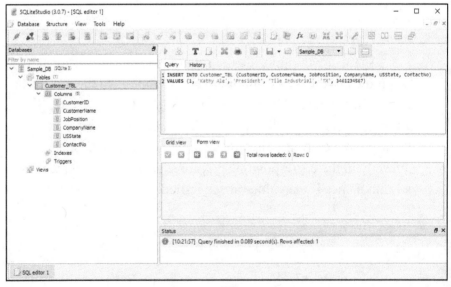

3. To check the new record of data inserted in the table, double-click **Customer_TBL** under the *TABLES* section at the left pane. Click the *DATA* tab at the right pane (between the *STRUCTURE* and *CONSTRAINTS* tabs). The table should be similar to what is shown below:

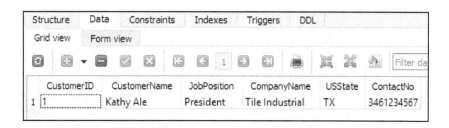

4. Click the *SQL EDITOR* option 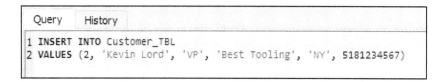 at the bottom left corner of the screen. To add another record without indicating the column names, type the following lines inside the *QUERY* tab:

INSERT INTO Customer_TBL
VALUES (2, 'Kevin Lord', 'VP', 'Best Tooling', 'NY', 5181234567)

5. Click the *EXECUTE QUERY* button  again. If the order of the data values corresponds exactly to the order of the table's columns, then no errors will be displayed in the *Status Area*.

6. At the bottom left corner of the screen, click the *CUSTOMER_TBL (SAMPLE_DB)* option

    Customer_TBL (Sample_DB) . Click the *GRID VIEW* tab then the

    REFRESH TABLE DATA button (or press *F5* on the keyboard). You will notice the new record inserted to the table.

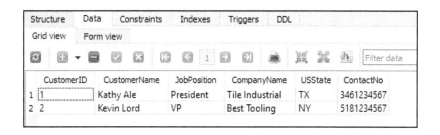

Inserting multiple rows of information gives an advantage if a number of records are needed to be stored in a table at a time. This is considered more efficient rather than inserting a single record at a time.

To insert two remaining records into the **Customer_TBL**:

1. Go to the *SQL EDITOR* and, without indicating the column names anymore, enter the following lines of codes:

```
INSERT INTO Customer_TBL
VALUES
(3, 'Kim Ash', 'Director', 'Car World', 'CA', 5101234567),
(4, 'Abby Karr', 'Manager', 'West Mart', 'NV', 7751234567)
```

2. Click the *EXECUTE QUERY* button .

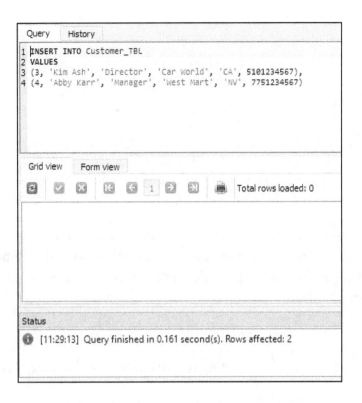

3. Go to the Customer_TBL (Sample_DB) option then click the *REFRESH TABLE DATA* button (or press F5 on the keyboard). The two records are now inserted to the database table.

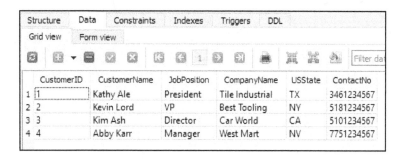

When we designed the **Customer_TBL** table in one of the previous chapters, the **JobPosition** field was defined to allow null values. This happens if the company obtains a new customer, but his job title is still unknown. Now, to add a new record without entering information for the **JobPosition** data field:

1. Type the following SQL lines, indicating the corresponding column names:

INSERT INTO Customer_TBL (CustomerID, CustomerName, CompanyName, USState, ContactNo)
VALUES (5, 'Mike Armhs', '1 Driving School', 'NJ', 2011234567)

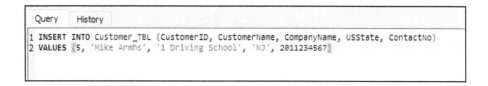

2. Click the *EXECUTE QUERY* button and then go to

   Customer_TBL (Sample_DB) option. Click the *REFRESH TABLE*

DATA button ⟳ (press F5 on the keyboard). Since no data was stored in the **JobPosition** field, it now displays NULL as the value.

	CustomerID	CustomerName	JobPosition	CompanyName	USState	ContactNo
1	1	Kathy Ale	President	Tile Industrial	TX	3461234567
2	2	Kevin Lord	VP	Best Tooling	NY	5181234567
3	3	Kim Ash	Director	Car World	CA	5101234567
4	4	Abby Karr	Manager	West Mart	NV	7751234567
5	5	Mike Armhs	NULL	1 Driving School	NJ	2011234567

UPDATE Statement

The SQL language always provides a way to update existing data stored in a database. Depending on the user requirements, data can be modified on one record or multiple records at a time using the UPDATE statement. Take note, only one table is updated at a time in a particular database. The standard syntax for this DML command is:

```
UPDATE TABLE_NAME
  SET column_1 = EXPRESSION_1,
      column_2 = EXPRESSION_2,
      ...
      column_n = EXPRESSION_N
[WHERE predicates];
```

The WHERE clause statement is optional and specifies which rows need to be updated. So, if the WHERE clause is not included then all the records of the table are automatically updated. Again, *"n"* represents the maximum number of columns. From the last example of the INSERT command statement, you added a customer record without providing data for the **JobPosition** field. Let's say you eventually found out that the contact person is the vice-president of the company, then you have to modify this existing record.

1. Click the [SQL editor 1] option to go back to the *SQL EDITOR* then type the following lines of code:

```
UPDATE Customer_TBL
SET JobPosition = 'VP'
WHERE CustomerName = 'Mike Armhs';
```

2. Click the *EXECUTE QUERY* button  to run the programming lines.

3. Click the Customer_TBL (Sample_DB) option then the *REFRESH TABLE DATA* button (press F5 on the keyboard). The value 'VP' under the **JobPosition** field is now indicated for the customer named Mike Armhs.

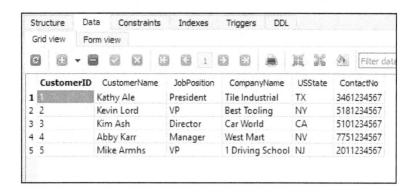

Some database users may find it more comprehensible if they see 'Vice-President' for a customer's job position instead of 'VP'. To update multiple customer records with 'VP' as the value for the **JobPosition** field at one time, execute the following lines of code:

1. At the bottom left corner of the screen, click the

   SQL editor 1

   option and modify the programming lines into the following:

UPDATE Customer_TBL
SET JobPosition = 'Vice-President'
WHERE JobPosition = 'VP';

2. Click the *EXECUTE QUERY* button .

```
Query    History

1 UPDATE Customer_TBL
2    SET JobPosition = 'Vice-President'
3    WHERE JobPosition = 'VP';
```

3. To update the values of the table, click the

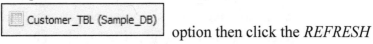 option then click the *REFRESH*

TABLE DATA button (press F5 on the keyboard). The
'VP' value has now been changed to 'Vice-President'.

DELETE Statement

This DML command will remove data records from a particular table but not the table itself. This happens when certain database information is not needed anymore, either they are already outdated, or people have no use for them at all. Removing unwanted data from the system can free up some storage space. The deletion of one record, multiple records or even all the records of the table at one time is accomplished through the execution of the DELETE command statement. Kindly take note that this removes an entire row or a full record, and not just values from a specific column. Extreme caution should be exercised when performing this command because the effect of the DELETE statement could be permanent and data recovery may be impossible. Below is the standard syntax for this command:

DELETE FROM *TABLE_NAME*
[WHERE *CONDITION*];

When deleting selected rows of data from a table, you need to include the WHERE clause in the program execution. Without the WHERE clause, all the records will be removed from the table. To demonstrate how the DELETE statement works, you will first create a copy of the **Customer_TBL** table so the original table can be used for further exercises.

1. In the *DATABASE NAVIGATOR* pane right-click on **Customer_TBL**. Choose *CREATE A SIMILAR TABLE* from the given options.

83

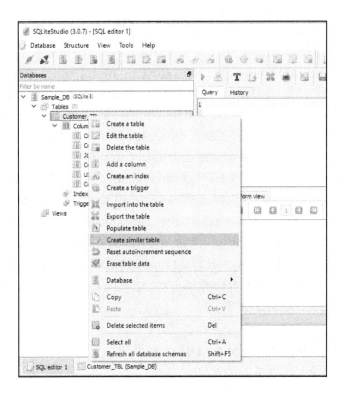

2. Provide a name for your table by tying **Customer_TBL2**
   inside the *TABLE NAME* input box.

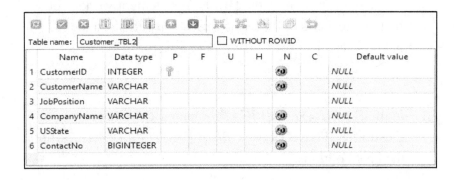

3. Under the *STRUCTURE* tab, click on the *COMMIT*

   STRUCTURE CHANGES button 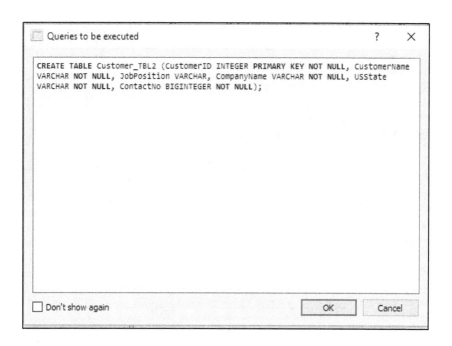 and you will get the
   screen below.

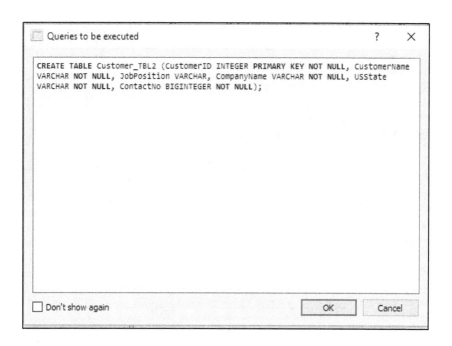

4. Click on the *OK* button and it will create a new
   Customer_TBL2 table, which will be used to demonstrate
   the DELETE command.

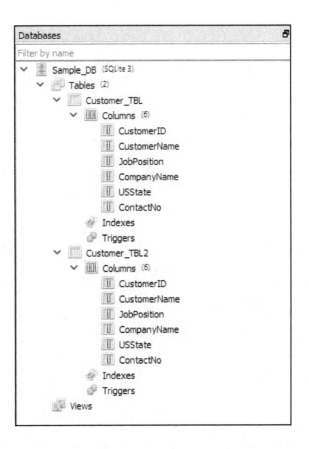

This new table is empty, so you will have to copy the records from **Customer_TBL** table by following the steps below:

1. To ensure that the data in the table is updated click the

   Customer_TBL (Sample_DB) option, then click the *REFRESH*

   TABLE DATA button (press F5 on the keyboard).

2. Click the space on top of the first row, just before the **CustomerID** column heading to highlight all the records in the table.

86

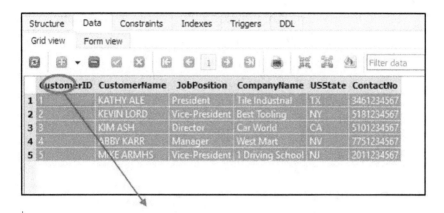

Click here to highlight all records.

3. Right-click on the first highlighted cell just under the
   CustomerID column then select the *COPY* option. This will
   copy all the values in the table.

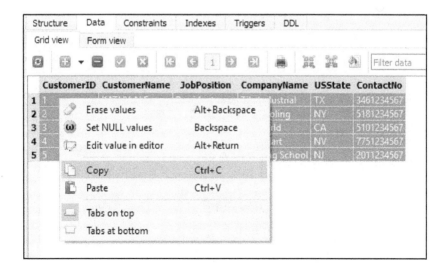

4. In the left pane, double-click on **Customer_TBL2**. Click on the *DATA* tab, then the *GRID VIEW* tab and the same column headings as in the original table are now displayed. The data you copied from the **Customer_TBL** table will be populated in this second table.

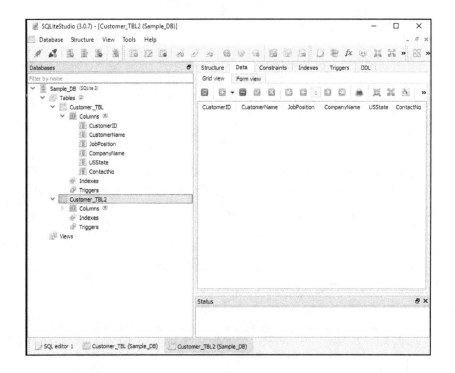

5. Below the *GRID VIEW* tab, click the dropdown arrow just beside the *INSERT ROW* button then select *INSERT MULTIPLE ROWS* option.

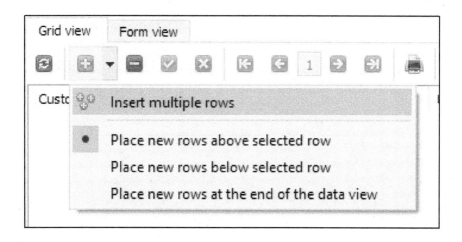

6. Type **5** inside the *NUMBER OF ROWS TO INSERT* input box then click OK.

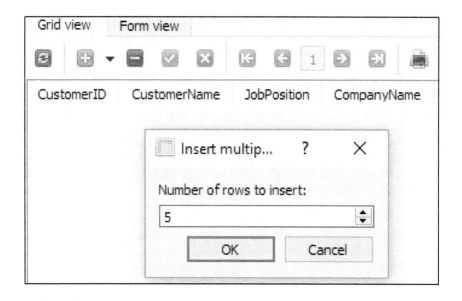

7. **Customer_TBL2** table will now have 5 rows of data, in which each field contains NULL values. This is where the data values copied from the **Customer_TBL** table will be inserted.

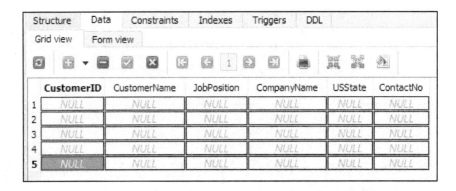

8. Right-click on the first cell and then choose *PASTE*.

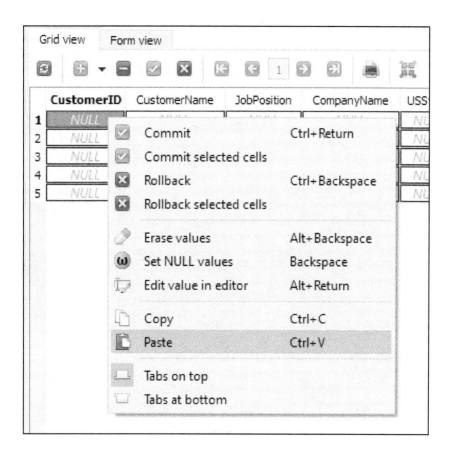

9. All the **Customer_TBL** data values will be copied and inserted into the new **Customer_TBL2** table, which will be used to demonstrate the function of the DELETE command.

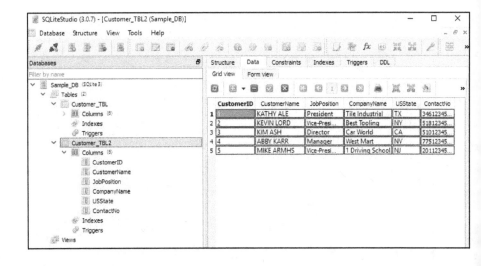

10. To save the data in the **Customer_TBL2** table, click on the

COMMIT STRUCTURE CHANGES button .

To delete a record where the customer's name matches to
'KATHY ALE' from the **Customer_TBL2** table:

1. Click the ⌐ SQL editor 1 option and type the following in the

QUERY tab. Click the *EXECUTE QUERY* button .

DELETE FROM Customer_TBL2
WHERE CustomerName = 'KATHY ALE';

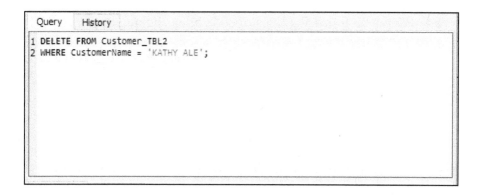

2. To check if the customer record of Kathy Ale has been deleted, open the **Customer_TBL2** table by clicking

    Customer_TBL2 (Sample_DB) option. To update the values,

    click on the *REFRESH TABLE DATA* button (or press F5 on the keyboard). You should notice that the customer record has already been deleted.

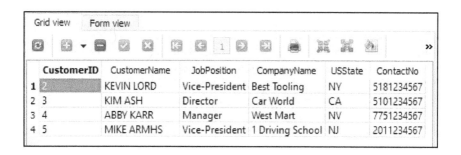

To delete more than one customer record from the **Customer_TBL2** table where the customer's position matches to 'Vice-President':

1. Type the following lines of code after clicking the 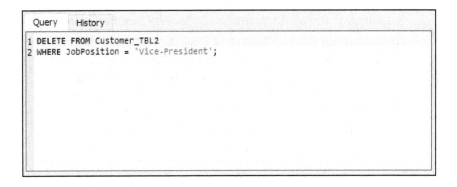 SQL editor 1 option, and then click the *EXECUTE QUERY* button .

> DELETE FROM Customer_TBL2
> WHERE JobPosition = 'Vice-President';

```
Query    History
1 DELETE FROM Customer_TBL2
2 WHERE JobPosition = 'Vice-President';
```

2. To check if the records have been deleted, click on the Customer_TBL2 (Sample_DB) option to go to the **Customer_TBL2** table. To update the information stored in the table, click on the *REFRESH TABLE DATA* button (or press **F5** on the keyboard). Notice that all the matching records have already been deleted.

To delete all the remaining records of **Customer_TBL2** table at one time:

1. Go to the *SQL EDITOR*, enter the following lines of code under the *QUERY* tab, and then click the *EXECUTE QUERY* button ▷ .

DELETE FROM Customer_TBL2

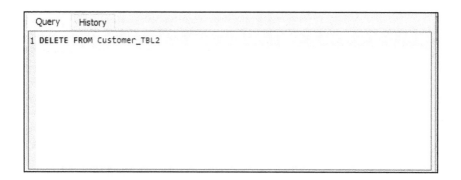

2. To check if all the records have been deleted from the **Customer_TBL2** table, click on ⬜ Customer_TBL2 (Sample_DB)

and then the *REFRESH TABLE DATA* button (press F5 on the keyboard) to update the values. You will notice that executing the single DELETE command has removed all the records from the table.

Data Control Language (DCL) Statement

Data Control Language (DCL) statements have the primary role of enforcing data security in a multi-user database environment. Only the database owner or administrator can provide or remove privileges on database objects. The two available DCL command statements are GRANT and REVOKE. Since this SQLite eBook focuses on a stand-alone personal database with a single user, only an overview of the syntax of these DCL statements will be discussed.

GRANT Statement

The SQL GRANT statement is a control command that provides database users the privilege or access in manipulating database objects.

Syntax:

GRANT *PRIVILEGE_NAME*
ON objectname
TO {user_name | PUBLIC | rolename}
[WITH GRANT OPTION];

- *PRIVILEGE_NAME* - the access right granted to a user that can be ALL, EXECUTE or SELECT
- objectname - the name of the database object such as a table or view
- username - the name of the user to whom the access right is granted
- PUBLIC - this is used to grant access rights to all users instead of specifying a particular user
- rolename - a set of privileges grouped together
- WITH GRANT OPTION - optional part of the command structure that permits the database user to grant access right to other users (use this carefully because you don't want this right to be abused by any user)

To grant a SELECT permission on the existing **Customer_TBL** table to a certain *user1*, use the following programming lines:

```
GRANT SELECT
ON Customer_TBL
TO user1;
```

REVOKE Statement

The SQL REVOKE statement is another control command that removes access rights or privileges from users in manipulating database objects.

Syntax:

```
REVOKE PRIVILEGE_NAME
ON objectname
FROM {user_name | PUBLIC | rolename};
```

To remove a SELECT permission on the existing **Customer_TBL** table from a certain *user1*, use the following lines of code:

```
REVOKE SELECT
ON Customer_TBL
FROM user1;
```

Chapter Summary

• There are different SQL commands that will help a user define, manipulate and control databases. They are further categorized into three groups: Data Definition Language (DDL), Data Manipulation Language (DML) and Data Control Language (DCL).

• The primary functions of the DDL commands are to create, destroy or change database objects. They include the following statements: CREATE, DROP and ALTER.

• The primary function of the DML commands is to manipulate database objects. They include the following statements: SELECT, INSERT, UPDATE and DELETE.

• The primary function of the DCL commands is to manage user privileges in accessing the database system. They include the following statements: GRANT and REVOKE.

In the next chapter you will learn normalization techniques in enhancing database designs to improve the system's efficiency in performing different database operations.

Chapter Six: Database Normalization

In this chapter you will learn an in-depth knowledge of normalization techniques and their importance in enhancing database conceptualization and design. As such, more efficient databases are created that will provide the SQL software application an edge in performing effective queries and maintaining data integrity all the time.

Definition and Importance of Database Normalization

Basically, normalization is the process of designing a database model to reduce data redundancy by breaking large tables into smaller but more manageable ones, where the same types of data are grouped together. What is the importance of database normalization? Normalizing a database ensures that pieces information stored are well organized, easily managed and always accurate with no unnecessary duplication. In the previous chapters, merging the data from the **CUSTOMER_TBL** table with the **ORDER_TBL** table will result into a large table that is not normalized:

ORDER ID	ORDER DATE	CUSTOMER ID	NAME	POSITION	COMPANY	STATE	CONTACT NO	PRODUCT ID	ORDER QTY
1	2016-05-23	1	Kathy Ale	President	Tile Industrial	TX	3461234567	4	300
2	2016-09-09	1	Kathy Ale	President	Tile Industrial	TX	3461234567	5	100
3	2016-02-17	3	Kim Ash	Director	Car World	CA	5101234567	2	150
4	2016-05-12	2	Kevin Lord	VP	Best Tooling	NY	5181234567	2	500

If you look closely into this table, there is data redundancy on the part of the customer named Kathy Ale. Always remember to minimize data redundancy to save disk or storage space and prevent users from getting confused with the amount of information the table contains. There is also a possibility that for every table containing such customer information, one table may not have the same matching information as with another. So how will a user verify which one is correct? Also, if a certain customer information needs to be updated, then you are required to update the data in all of the database tables where it is included. This entails wastage of time and effort in managing the entire database system.

Forms of Normalization

Normal form is the way of measuring the level to which a database has been normalized and there are three common normal forms:

First Normal Form (1NF)

The *first normal form* or *1NF* aims to divide a given set of data into logical units or tables of related information. Each table will have an assigned primary key, which is a specified column that uniquely identifies the table rows. Every cell should have a single value and each row of a certain table refers to a unique record of information. The columns that refer to the attributes of the table information are given unique names and consist of the same type of data values. Moreover, the columns and the rows are arranged is no particular order.

Let us add a new table named **Employee_TBL** to the database we started discussing in Chapter 3, which contains basic information about the company's employees:

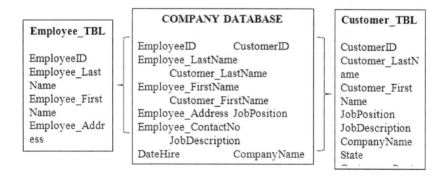

Based from the diagram above, the entire company database was divided into two tables – **Employee_TBL** and **Customer_TBL**. *EmployeeID* and *CustomerID* are the primary keys set for these tables respectively. By doing this, database information is easier to read and manage as compared to just having one big table consisting of so many columns and rows. The data values stored in **Employee_TBL** table only refer to the pieces of information describing the company's employees while those that pertain exclusively to the company's customers are contained in the **Customer_TBL** table.

Second Normal Form (2NF)

The *second normal form* or *2NF* is the next step after you are successfully done with the first normal form. This process now focuses on the functional dependency of the database, which describes the relationships existing between attributes. When there is an attribute that determines the value of another, then a functional dependency exists between them. Thus, you will store data values from the **Employee_TBL** and **Customer_TBL** tables, which are partly dependent on the assigned primary keys, into separate tables.

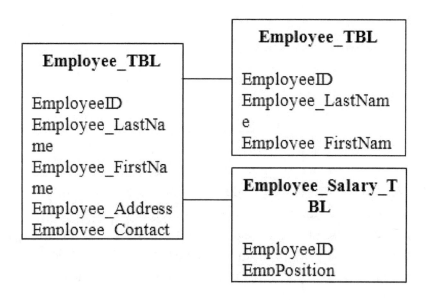

Employee_TBL

EmployeeID
Employee_LastName
Employee_FirstName
Employee_Address
Employee_Contact

Employee_TBL

EmployeeID
Employee_LastNam
e
Employee_FirstNam

**Employee_Salary_T
BL**

EmployeeID
EmpPosition

In the figure above, the attributes that are partly dependent on the *EmployeeID* primary key have been removed from **Employee_TBL**, and are now stored in a new table called **Employee_Salary_TBL**. The attributes that were kept in the original table are completely dependent on the table's primary key, which means for every record of last name, first name, address and contract number there is a corresponding unique particular employee ID. Unlike in the **Employee_Salary_TBL** table, a particular employee ID does not point to a unique employee position nor salary rate. It is possible that there could be more than one employee that holds the same position (EmpPosition), and receives the same amount of pay rate (Payrate) or bonus (Bonus).

Third Normal Form (3NF)

In the *third normal form* or *3NF*, pieces of information that are completely not dependent on the primary key should still be separated from the database table. Looking back at the **Customer_TBL**, two attributes are totally independent of the **CustomerID** primary key - **JobPosition** (job position) and **JobDescription** (job position description). Regardless of who the customer is, any job position will have the same duties and responsibilities. Thus, the two attributes will be separated into another table called **Position_TBL**.

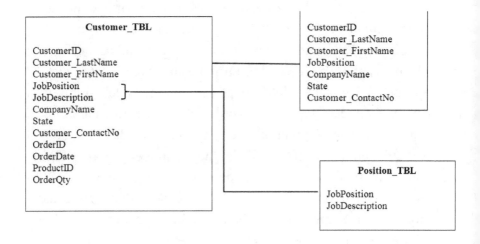

Drawbacks of Normalization

Though database normalization has presented a number of advantages in organizing, simplifying and maintaining the integrity of databases, you still need to consider the following disadvantages:

- Creating more tables to spread out data increases the need to join tables and such task becomes more tedious, which makes the database harder to conceptualize.
- Instead of real and meaningful data, database tables will contain lines of codes.
- Query processes becomes extremely difficult since the database model is getting too complex.
- Database performance is reduced or becomes slower as the normal form type progresses.
- A normalized database requires much more CPU and memory usage.
- To execute the normalization process efficiently, the user needs the appropriate knowledge and skills in optimizing databases. Otherwise, the design will be filled with inconsistencies.

Chapter Summary

- Database normalization is the process of optimizing database designs by organizing tables to avoid redundancy of data.
- Since normalization eliminates the duplication of data, the database is simplified and can easily be managed.
- The different forms of normalization are the first normal form (1NF), second normal form (2NF) and the third normal form (3NF).
- Normalizing databases also have some drawbacks, such as reduced database performances, increased CPU and memory usage, harder database conceptualization, and more complicated query processes.

In the next chapter you will learn how to maintain database integrity using the various SQL transaction tools.

Chapter Seven: Database Transactions

In this chapter you will learn how to use three of the common SQL transaction commands using SQLiteStudio – COMMIT, ROLLBACK and SAVEPOINT. Controlling such transactions entails the user to manage certain database changes that are usually brought about by the DML commands (insert, update and delete).

When a database transaction has been successfully executed, the table's data or structure will definitely be altered. During a transaction execution, information is going to be stored in a temporary database space or what is called a *rollback area*. To finalize these transactions and permanently save the changes made to the database, execute the appropriate transaction command. It is only after this process that the *rollback area* is emptied.

COMMIT Command

The SQL COMMIT statement is responsible for saving all the transactions into a database. You have already encountered this command in Chapter 6 through the *COMMIT CHANGES STRUCTURE* button (when a copy of the **Customer_TBL** table was created). Now, using SQLiteStudio, you will manipulate the

Customer_TBL table structure by adding a new record in the *GRID VIEW* mode.

1. Go to the *SQL EDITOR* by clicking the ⬚ SQL editor 1 option. To end all the transactions currently running in the database, enter the following programming line in the *QUERY* tab and click the *EXECUTE QUERY* button ▷ :

END TRANSACTION;

2. Double-click **Customer_TBL** table in the *DATABASE NAVIGATOR* pane, under the *TABLES* list. Make sure that the *GRID* view is displayed by clicking the *DATA* tab at the right. All the records of the **Customer_TBL** table are now displayed.

3. Click the cell containing **CustomerID = 5**, which is the last row of the first column in the table.

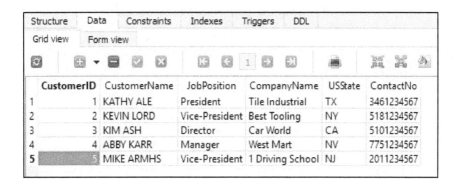

4. Choose the *PLACE NEW ROWS BELOW SELECTED ROW* option from the dropdown arrow that is beside the *INSERT ROW (INS)* button.

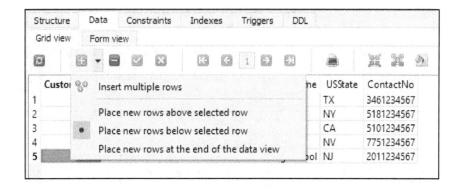

5. To see the new empty row added to the table, click the
   INSERT ROW (INS) button.

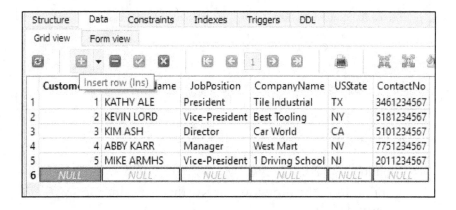

6. Add the data values below in the new table record:

CustomerID: 6
CustomerName: JOHN DEPP
JobPosition: President
CompanyName: Rockers Mine Company
USState: TX
ContactNo: 3467654321

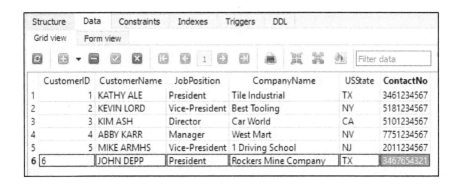

7. To permanently store the new data values added, click

   the COMMIT button .

ROLLBACK Command

The SQL ROLLBACK statement is the reverse of the COMMIT command, where all the unsaved changes will be discarded. However, transactions can only be undone since the last COMMIT or ROLLBACK statement that was executed.

113

Syntax:

ROLLBACK [WORK];

In addition, before a ROLLBACK command can be performed, make sure that the transactions have already started.

Syntax:

BEGIN TRANSACTION;

To demonstrate in SQLiteStudio how a ROLLBACK statement works, you will modify the DROP TABLE command:

1. Click the ⎘ SQL editor 1 option and go to the *QUERY* tab. Enter the following programming line and then click the *EXECUTE QUERY* button ▶ :

   BEGIN TRANSACTION;

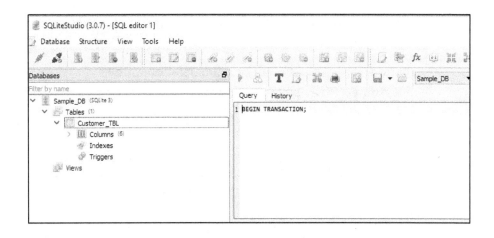

2. Go back to the SQL EDITOR and clear out the *QUERY* tab. This time, type the following code and then click the

   EXECUTE QUERY button 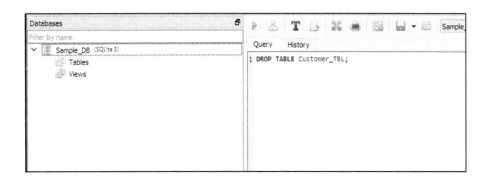. This will remove the **Customer_TBL** table from the *TABLES* list.

   DROP TABLE Customer_TBL;

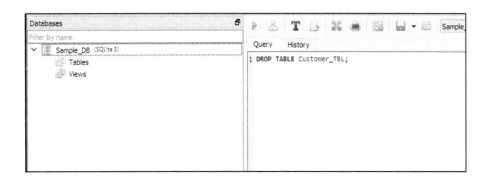

3. Erase the content of the *QUERY* tab again and type the following command statement. Click the *EXECUTE QUERY* button 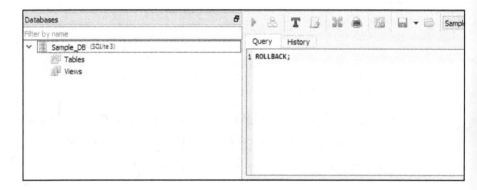 . This will reverse the deletion of the **Customer_TBL** table.

ROLLBACK;

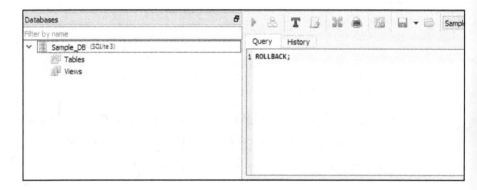

4. To check if the execution of the ROLLBACK command was successful, right-click anywhere inside the *DATABASE NAVIGATOR* pane then select *REFRESH ALL DATABASE SCHEMAS* option.

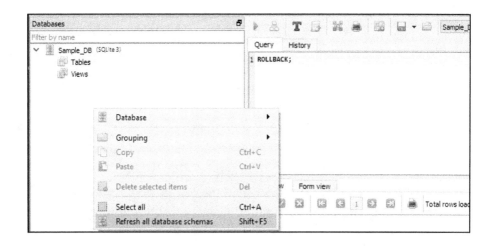

5. Now, click the *TABLE* list at the left pane to see that the **Customer_TBL** table should be back again.

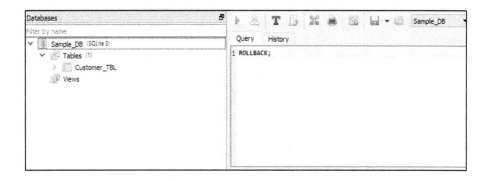

SAVEPOINT Command

The SQL SAVEPOINT statement is performed when you want to reverse a particular transaction just back to a certain point and not the entire database transaction. This is executed before a ROLLBACK action. In this way, you will be able to manage several transactions into smaller groups of SQL commands.

Syntax:

SAVEPOINT *SAVEPOINT_NAME*;

You can also use the SAVEPOINT and the ROLLBACK commands together.

Syntax:

ROLLBACK TO *SAVEPOINT_NAME*;

The name of the database object (to which the SQL transactions will be performed) can be used as a savepoint name. However, they should be different from the group of transactions that you want to break down into several points (or *segments*). To demonstrate how a SAVEPOINT with a ROLLBACK command works, delete some records from the **Customer_TBL** table first and reverse this database transaction.

1. Click the ☐ SQL editor 1 option and type the code below in the *QUERY* tab. click the *EXECUTE QUERY* button ▷ :

BEGIN TRANSACTION;

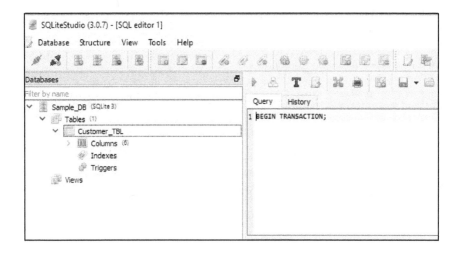

2. Delete all the contents of the *QUERY* tab, type the following code and click the *EXECUTE QUERY* button ▷ . This will create a savepoint section before deleting the last record of the **Customer_TBL** table.

SAVEPOINT Customer_SP1;

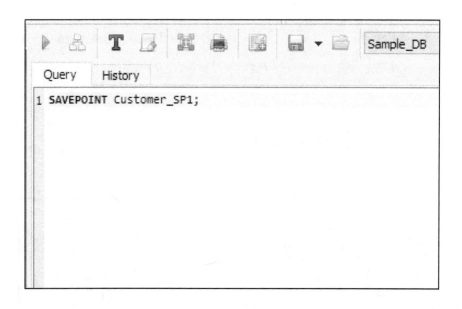

3. To remove the last record of the **Customer_TBL** table, clear out the *QUERY* tab again. Then type the following programming line and click the *EXECUTE QUERY* button ▶ :

DELETE FROM Customer_TBL WHERE CustomerID = 6;

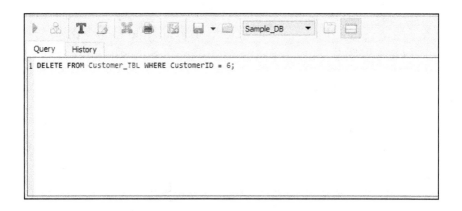

4. To check if the record was removed, double-click
   Customer_TBL table under the *TABLES* list in the
   DATABASE NAVIGATOR pane at the left. Click the *DATA*
   tab at the right and go to the *GRID VIEW* tab. Then click the

   REFRESH TABLE DATA button 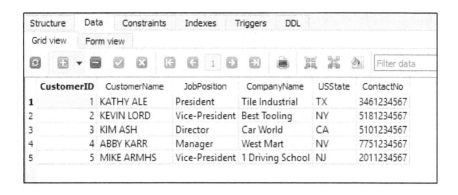 (press F5 on the
   keyboard). You should see a table that looks like the
   following:

CustomerID	CustomerName	JobPosition	CompanyName	USState	ContactNo
1	1 KATHY ALE	President	Tile Industrial	TX	3461234567
2	2 KEVIN LORD	Vice-President	Best Tooling	NY	5181234567
3	3 KIM ASH	Director	Car World	CA	5101234567
4	4 ABBY KARR	Manager	West Mart	NV	7751234567
5	5 MIKE ARMHS	Vice-President	1 Driving School	NJ	2011234567

5. Now, click the 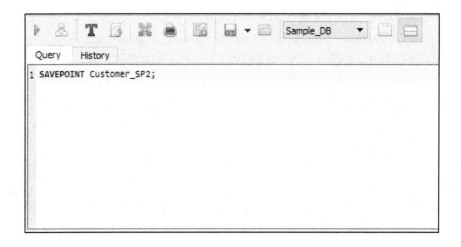 SQL editor 1 option again and empty the *QUERY* tab. Then type the following programming line and click the *EXECUTE QUERY* button ▶ , to create the second savepoint section (this is created before deleting the record where the **CustomerID=5**).

SAVEPOINT Customer_SP2;

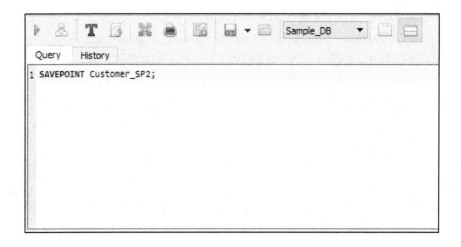

6. Delete the customer record where the **CustomerID=5** by clearing out the *QUERY* tab and typing the following line of code. Then click the EXECUTE QUERY button ▶ :

DELETE FROM Customer_TBL WHERE CustomerID=5;

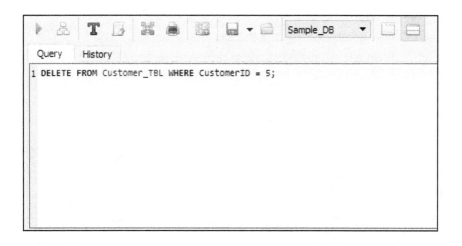

7. Check if the customer record was deleted by clicking the 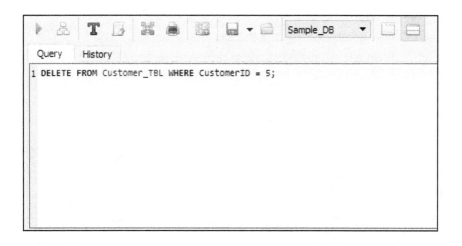 Customer_TBL (Sample_DB) option at the bottom left corner of the screen. Click the *DATA* tab at the right and under the *GRID VIEW* tab, click the *REFRESH TABLE DATA* button (press F5 from the keyboard). The table you will see should be the same as the following:

	CustomerID	CustomerName	JobPosition	CompanyName	USState	ContactNo
1	1	KATHY ALE	President	Tile Industrial	TX	3461234567
2	2	KEVIN LORD	Vice-President	Best Tooling	NY	5181234567
3	3	KIM ASH	Director	Car World	CA	5101234567
4	4	ABBY KARR	Manager	West Mart	NV	7751234567

8. Now, reversing the last transaction done, click the [SQL editor 1] option again and erase everything inside the *QUERY* tab. After typing the following programming line, click the

   EXECUTE QUERY button ▶ :

   ROLLBACK TO Customer_SP2;

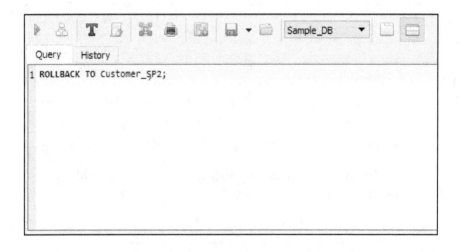

9. To see if the deleted record has been reversed, click

   [Customer_TBL (Sample_DB)] and then the *DATA* tab located at the right. Click the *GRID VIEW* tab and the *REFRESH TABLE*

   DATA button ⟳ (press F5 from the keyboard). Your table should contain the same data values as the one below:

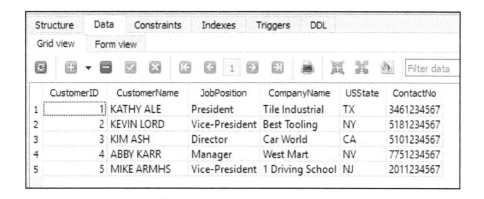

10. To reverse transaction where a record was first deleted, clear the *QUERY* tab, enter the following programming line and then click the *EXECUTE QUERY* button 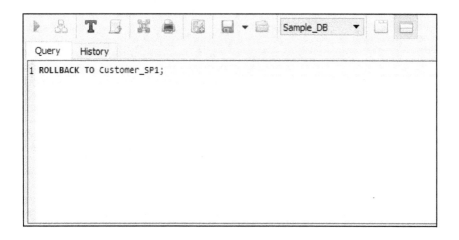 :

ROLLBACK TO Customer_SP1;

11. Verifying if the record deletion was reversed, click the
    ▢ Customer_TBL (Sample_DB) option and then click the *DATA* tab at
    the right pane. Go to the *GRID VIEW* tab and then click the
    REFRESH TABLE DATA button ▢ (press F5 on the
    keyboard). The table should look exactly as the original one,
    before any of the deletion transactions have occurred.

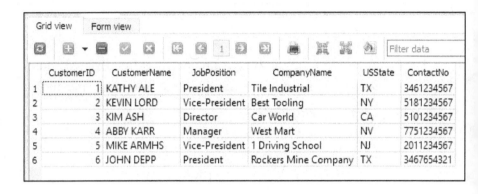

Chapter Summary

- The SQL transaction commands that help manage changes in the databases performed by a user are COMMIT, ROLLBACK and SAVEPOINT.
- The SQL COMMIT statement is used to permanently save all the changes done by certain database transactions.
- The SQL ROLLBACK statement is used to discard all unsaved modifications performed by the user to a database.
- The SQL SAVEPOINT statement is used to mark or save a current point in the processing of a transaction, assisting the user in managing numerous transactions to smaller groups of SQL commands.

In the next chapter you will learn the various database operators and their importance in enhancing database processes.

Chapter Eight: Database Operators

In this chapter you will learn what an operator is and the available database operators in SQL. You will also be introduced on how to properly use various operators in your data querying needs.

An SQL operator is a reserved word or character used mainly within the SELECT command statement's WHERE clause. Its primary function is to perform a given operation, such as a comparison or an arithmetic process. It can also be used to specify a certain SQL statement condition or serve as a conjunction for multiple conditions. In this chapter, we will focus on the following categories of operators: mathematical (or arithmetic), comparison and logical operators.

Mathematical or Arithmetic Operators

Like in any other computer languages, the main job of a mathematical or arithmetic operator is to perform an SQL mathematical function. Below is a table of the five core mathematical operators in SQLite:

OPERATOR	DESCRIPTON	EXAMPLE
+	Addition (adds two numbers)	a + b
-	Subtraction (subtracts two numbers)	a - b
*	Multiplication (multiples two numbers)	a * b
/	Division (divides two numbers)	a / b
%	Division with remainder (divides two numbers but returns the remainder)	a % b

These mathematical operators can be combined with one another. Just remember the rules of precedence: multiplication and division operations are performed first and then followed by addition and subtraction. Also take note that a mathematical expression surrounded by parentheses should be evaluated as a block.

Comparison Operators

The role of a comparison operator is to test single values in an SQL statement and will result to a true (1) or false (0) value, depending on the comparative evaluation. Let us assume that a = 10 and b = 20. The table below summarizes how the comparison operators can be used and the corresponding results.

OPERATOR	DESCRIPTION	EXAMPLE	RESULT
= and ==	Equality (checks if two values are equal)	a = b	0 (false)
!= and < >	Non-Equality (checks if two values are not equal)	a != b a < > b	1 (true)
>	Greater Than (checks if the value on the left is greater than the value on the right)	a > b	0 (false)
<	Less Than (checks if the value on the left is less than the value on the right)	a < b	1 (true)
> =	Greater Than or Equal To (checks if the value on the left is greater than or equal to the value on the right)	a > = b	0 (false)
< =	Less Than or Equal To (checks if the value on the left is less than or equal to the value on the right)	a < = b	1 (true)

The greater than and the less than operators are the two most commonly used comparison operators. They can be combined with the equal sign as shown in the last two rows of the table above.

Logical Operators

Logical operators use different SQL keywords to perform comparisons instead of symbols. They also allow Boolean expressions to be combined, which means they can perform more conditional operations. Let us take the following as examples:

a = true (1) and b = false (0)   x = 10 and y = 20

OPERATOR	DESCRIPTION	EXAMPLE	RESULT
AND	checks for all Boolean expressions to be true	a AND b	0 (false)
OR	checks for any Boolean expressions to be true	a OR b	1 (true)
BETWEEN	checks if a value inclusively falls inside a range	x BETWEEN 1 and y	1 (true)
IN	checks if a value is in a list of values	x IN (1, 5, 7)	0 (false)
NOT	negates and flips a Boolean expression's value	x NOT IN (1, 5, 7)	1 (true)
IS NULL	checks if a value is null	x IS NULL	0 (false)
IS NOT NULL	checks if a value is not null	x IS NOT NULL	1 (true)

Chapter Summary

- A reserved word or character, an SQL database operator is used to perform a given operation within the SELECT command statement's WHERE clause.
- Mathematical or arithmetic operators are used to perform mathematical functions that involve the four basic operations (addition, subtraction, multiplication and division).
- Comparison operators test single values in an SQL statement, resulting to a true (1) or a false (0) value after the evaluation.
- Logical operators use SQL keywords in performing comparisons that allow Boolean expressions to be combined to evaluate more conditional operations

In the next chapter you will learn what database security is and its importance in managing the entire database system.

Chapter Nine: Database Security

In this chapter you will learn the basics of database security - its definition, importance and how to manage the users who are allowed to access the system. Security factors should be taken into consideration even at the start of conceptualizing the database model. It becomes a full-time job when administering privileges and security has started, which is often performed by database administrators (DBAs). However, it becomes a complex issue to address especially when excessive security policies create bureaucracy in an organization. That is why you need to have a clear picture of the answers to the following security questions:

- Who is allowed to access the database system?
- Is the database system critical to the organization's operations?
- What are the backup plans available in the event of a database failure?
- Are there security measures implemented in case the database will be available for web applications?
- Should changes to the tables be logged into the system?

Database Security Definition

Database security is basically defined as the process of protecting data from unauthorized access, which also includes the act of implementing protocols to prevent unauthorized connectivity and manage distribution of user privileges. Bear in mind that many users exist who need to connect and use the database system - creators, administrators, programmers and end users, among others. Generally, the DBA assigns each user a particular user account and password that will give him the access to the database. The given password should be changed immediately by the user since that will be his confidential and personal information. Also, the DBA does not need to know what the user's password is.

Database Security Importance

Managing security at different levels of user access is essential since databases usually contain sensitive information that should not be available to everyone in an organization. The DBA controls which database operations can be performed and what part of the database can be accessed by each authorized user. Thus, the most important reason for implementing database security is data protection against intentional or unintentional threats. Such data loss or corruption could possibly bring about drastic effects to the daily operations of an organization. Just imagine if a bank would compromise thousands of customers' credit card information, it would surely be devastating for the company's credibility and stability.

Another aspect of database security is to prevent data tampering or modification in a distributed environment ,where data continuously flows. In the case of a modification attack, an unauthorized user on a database network will intercept the data being transferred and changes it before it is re-transmitted. An example is changing the amount of an electronic bank transfer from $100 to $1,000. How much more risk is at stake, if a certain business organization, transfers thousands, or even millions of dollars?

Also, it becomes more feasible for a database user to falsify an identity in a network environment just to gain access to confidential information. Such culprits can attempt to steal personal information like another person's social security and driver's license numbers, and then setup a fake credit card account in someone else's name. In this case, the DBA should be able to monitor the activities of the different database users and ensure that they will be held responsible for their actions.

Managing Database Privileges

You have already encountered privileges in Chapter 2, during the discussion of the DCL command statements (GRANT and REVOKE). To clearly define privileges, these are authority levels used to gain database access that further give permission to access the available objects, manipulate data and perform various administrative functions within the database. Like what was explained before, the GRANT command issues such privileges while the REVOKE command takes them away.

When a user is able to connect to a database, it does not mean that he can automatically access the data within the database. It is through these two types of database privileges that a user will be able to determine if he is allowed to perform data manipulation:

System Privileges

These are the type of privileges that permit database users to perform administrative functions within the database, which could result in drastic repercussions if not monitored carefully. System privileges also vary greatly among the different database software vendors, so you have to check first that they will be correctly implemented. The database administrative functions include the following:

- o Create and drop databases
- o Create and drop user accounts
- o Drop and alter the state of database objects

Object Privileges

These are the type of privileges that give users permission to perform certain operations on database objects. The owner of the existing database objects are the ones who could grant object privileges to the other system users. If you are an owner of an object, you are automatically granted all the privileges that are associated to that object you have created. The operations that can be performed on database objects include:

o Use a specific domain

o Access a specific table

o Insert data into a column or all the columns of a specific table

o Update a column or all the columns of a specific table

o Reference a column or all the columns of a specific table

Chapter Summary

- Database security is the process of implementing protocols that protect data from unauthorized access.

- Managing database security is accomplished in different levels to prevent loss, tampering and falsification of information.

- A privilege is the authority level used to gain database access that will further allow a user to manipulate the objects and data available in the system. It is classified into two types: system privileges and object privileges.

- System privileges govern the permissions granted to database users in performing administrative functions within the database. On the other hand, object privileges allow users to manipulate database objects.

In the next chapter you will learn how to enhance your query processes using all the available SQLite command statements

Chapter Ten: Maximizing Database Queries

In this chapter you will learn how to maximize the use of the available query command statements in SQLite to retrieve data from database tables. You will also be able to summarize, group and sort data when requesting and displaying significant database information.

Queries are valid inquiries into the database to retrieve and display relevant information, depending on the user's request. The main challenge is to correctly instruct the computer using SQL commands on what data to search for by manipulating the various database objects. The most basic form of an SQL query is using the SELECT statement. If you want to specify which table rows you want to select the data from, you will have to add certain conditions through the use of clauses. One of these clauses is the WHERE clause, which you have already encountered in one of the previous chapters during the discussion of the DML commands.

Sorting Data

Displaying and sorting data in a particular way requires the ORDER BY clause at the end of the SQL SELECT statement. The main function of this clause is to arrange information using a specific order, whether ascending or descending. By default, the individual table rows are sorted in an ascending order. So, to arrange records in a descending order, include the DESC operator right after the ORDER BY clause.

Syntax:

SELECT *COLUMN LIST*
FROM *TABLE_NAME*
ORDER BY *COLUMN_LIST* [ASC | DESC];

Perform the following steps to retrieve all customer records from the **Customer_TBL** table and display them by US state in ascending order:

1. Click the SQL editor 1 option to open the *SQL EDITOR*, type the following programming lines and then click the

   EXECUTE QUERY button .

   SELECT *
   FROM Customer_TBL
   ORDER BY USState;

2. Check the results displayed inside the *GRID VIEW* tab.

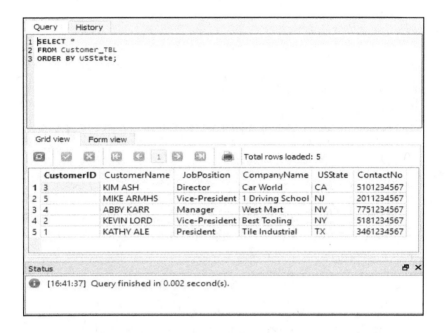

Since it was not specified how the records will be sorted, the records were arranged alphabetically (or in an ascending order) using the data values in the **USState** column. To sort the records in descending order, modify the programming code into the following:

1. Add *DESC* after **USState** in the *ORDER BY* clause inside the *QUERY* tab and then click the *EXECUTE QUERY* button

   ▷

   SELECT *
   FROM Customer_TBL
   ORDER BY USState DESC;

2. Take note of the changes in the results displayed inside the *GRID VIEW* tab.

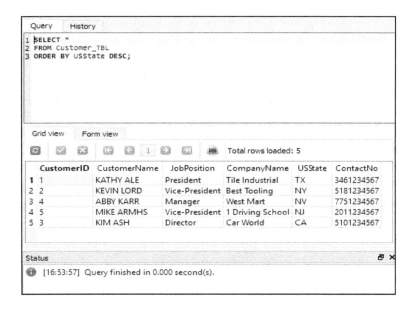

Grouping Data

If sorting data is querying the database and returning information in an organized fashion, then grouping data is combining columns with identical values in a logical order. This is accomplished through the use of the GROUP BY clause, which is similar to the terms aggregating, summarizing and rolling up. To demonstrate, we will identify how many customers are there for every job position in the **Customer_TBL** table by counting the number of data records and displaying the total number of customers per job position.

1. Type the following lines of code in the *SQL EDITOR* and

    then click the *EXECUTE QUERY* button ▶ :

```
SELECT JobPosition, COUNT(*) AS number_of_record
FROM Customer_TBL
GROUP BY JobPosition;
```

2. The result of this SELECT command combined with the GROUP BY clause is displayed inside the *GRID VIEW* tab.

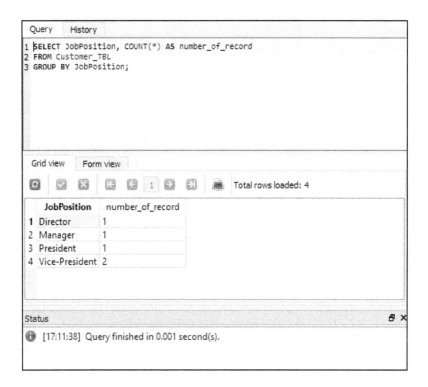

In this GROUP BY clause example, the data in the **JobPosition** column is retrieved and for each value occurrence, a record is counted with the use of the COUNT function. The **number_of_record** is a new column created that displayed the total number of records per job position. The Director, Manager and President positions have one record each while the Vice-President has two. This is because there are two customers who are vice-presidents (Kevin Lord and Mike Armhs). Furthermore, the records are sorted in an ascending order by default.

Summarizing Data

In the last SQL programming example, the COUNT function was introduced to arrange data results in groups. This is more popularly known as an aggregate function that can summarize data records. Basically, functions are SQL keywords that manipulate values within columns to produce the desired output required by the user. The following is a list of the common SQL aggregate functions used together with the GROUP BY statement (x denotes the column name where the function will be performed):

- COUNT(x) – counts how many non-null values exist in a specific column

- COUNT(*) – counts the number of records in a specific table

- AVG(x) – computes for the average of all the column values (null values excluded)

- MAX(x) – computes for the maximum value in the column (null values excluded)

- MIN(x) - computes for the minimum value in the column (null values excluded)

- SUM(x) – computes for the sum of the values in the column (null values are ignored)

Chapter Summary

- Maximizing database queries requires the knowledge of sorting, grouping and summarizing data records.
- The SORT BY clause is included when using the SQL SELECT statement to query and display data records in an ascending or descending order.
- The GROUP BY clause is included when using the SQL SELECT statement to query and organize data records by combining columns with identical values in a logical order.
- Aggregate functions are used together with the GROUP BY clause to retrieve and summarize information from database tables.

In the next chapter you will learn some advance topics as supplemental to the SQL knowledge that have already been introduced to you. They include an overview of cursors, triggers and errors, which could possibly assist you in extending the features of your SQL implementations.

Chapter Eleven: Supplementary Topics

In this chapter you will learn an overview of some advanced SQL topics that can extend your basic database operations, such as designing database structures, querying data and manipulating values. These advanced features are common in most SQL platforms to provide enhancements to your database applications.

Cursors

In general, SQL commands manipulate, or work around, database objects using set-based operations, meaning transactions are performed on a block or group of data. A cursor, on the other hand, retrieves and processes a subset of data from the database one row at a time. It is actually like a pointer that refers to a specific table row. When cursor is activated, a user can select, update or delete the row at which it is pointing. It also enables the SQL program to retrieve table rows one at a time and send it to a procedural code for processing. In this way, the entire table is processed row by row.

To use the cursor functionality, its existence is declared first using a compound statement that could also be destroyed upon exit. The following is the standard syntax for declaring a cursor (but may differ for every SQL implementation):

Syntax:

DECLARE CURSOR *CURSOR_NAME*
IS {*SELECT_STATEMENT*}

After the cursor has been declared or defined, the following operations can now be performed:

- **Opening a Cursor -** Once declared, the OPEN operation can be executed to gain access to the cursor, followed by the specified SELECT statement. The results of the database query will be saved in a certain area in the memory. The following is the standard format of the syntax when opening a cursor:

OPEN *CURSOR_NAME*;

- **Fetching Data from a Cursor -** The FETCH statement is executed if the query results are to be retrieved after opening the cursor. The following is the standard syntax for fetching data from a cursor:

FETCH NEXT FROM *CURSOR_NAME* [INTO *FETCH_LIST*]

The statement inside the square brackets is optional, which will let you allocate the data fetched into a particular variable.

- **Closing a Cursor** - There is a corresponding CLOSE statement that can be executed when you have opened a particular cursor. All the names and resources used will be released once the cursor has been closed. Thus, it is no longer available or usable in the program. The following is the standard syntax when a cursor is to be closed:

CLOSE *CURSOR_NAME*

Triggers

Sometimes there are cases when certain SQL operations or transactions need to occur after performing some specific actions. This is a scenario that describes an SQL statement triggering another one to take place. A trigger is simply an SQL procedure compiled in the database that executes certain transactions based on previously occurring transactions. Such triggers can be performed before or after executing a DML statement (INSERT, DELETE and UPDATE). Moreover, triggers can validate the integrity of data, maintain consistency of information, undo certain transactions, log operations, read and modify data values in different databases.

- **Creating a Trigger** - Once a trigger has been created, it cannot be altered or modified anymore (you can just either re-create or replace it). How a trigger works depends on what conditions are specified – whether it will be executed all at once when a DML statement is performed or it will be run multiple times for each table row that is affected by the given DML statement. A threshold value or a Boolean condition can also be included, which will trigger a course of action when the specified condition is met.

The standard syntax for creating a trigger is:

CREATE TRIGGER *TRIGGER_NAME*
TRIGGER_ACTION_TIMETRIGGER_EVENT
ON *TABLE_NAME*
[REFERENCING *OLD_OR_NEW_VALUE_ALIAS_LIST*]
TRIGGERED_ACTION

TRIGGER_NAME - the trigger's unique identifying name

TRIGGER_ACTION_TIMETRIGGER_EVENT - the specified time or duration that the set of triggered actions will occur (either before or after the triggering event).

TABLE_NAME – the database table for which the DML statements have been specified

TRIGGERED_ACTION – indicates the actions to be performed once an event is triggered

- **Dropping a Trigger**

The basic syntax for dropping or destroying a trigger is the same as dropping a table:

DROP TRIGGER *TRIGGER_NAME*;

Errors

Achieving an error-free implementation or design is considered to be one of the ultimate goals in handling any programming language. A database user can commit errors by simply performing inappropriate naming conventions, writing improperly the programming syntax (typographical errors like a missing apostrophe/parenthesis) or even when the data value entered does not correspond to the data type being defined.

To simplify things, SQL has created a way to return error messages so that users or programmers will be aware of what is happening in the database system. This will further lead to taking corrective measures to improve the situation. Some of the common error-handling features are the WHENEVER clause and the SQLSTATE status parameter.

SQLSTATE

The host variable or status parameter SQLSTATE is one of the SQL error-handling tools that includes a wide selection of anomalous programming conditions. It is a five-character string that consists of uppercase letters from A to Z and numeral values from 0 to 9. The first two characters refer to the class code, while the next three signify the subclass code. The indicated class code is responsible for identifying the status after an SQL statement has been completed – whether it is successful or not. If the execution of the SQL statement is not successful, then one of the major types of error conditions will be returned. Additional information about the execution of the SQL statement is also indicated in the subclass code.

The SQLSTATE is always updated after every operation. If its value is set to *'00000'*, this means that the execution was successful, and you can proceed to the succeeding operation. If it contains a string other than the five zeroes, then the user has to check his programming codes to correct the error committed. There are multiple ways on how to handle a certain SQL error, which normally depends on the on the class and subclass codes indicated by the SQLSTATE.

WHENEVER Clause

Another error-handling mechanism tool, the WHENEVER clause focuses on execution exceptions. Through this, an error is acknowledged and provides the programmer an option to rectify it. This is a lot better instead of not doing anything if an error occurs. If you cannot correct or reverse the error that was committed, then the application program can just be gracefully terminated.

The WHENEVER clause should be written before the executable part of the SQL code, in the declaration section to be exact. The standard syntax for the said clause is:

WHENEVER *CONDITION ACTION*;

CONDITION – the value can either be set to *'SQLERROR'* (will return TRUE if the class code value is not equivalent to *00, 01* or *02*) or *'NOT FOUND'* (will return TRUE if the SQLSTATE value is equivalent to 02000)

ACTION – the value can either be set to *'CONTINUE'* (program execution is continued as per normal) or *'GOTO address'* (a designated program address is executed)

Chapter Summary

- The SQL programming language provides advanced features that will enhance database structures, data querying operations and value manipulation, among others. These include cursors, triggers and errors.

- Cursors work as a pointer that refers to a specific table row. It enables the SQL program to retrieve and process table rows one at a time.

- Triggers are SQL procedures compiled in the database that perform certain transactions based on previously occurring transactions.

- Error-handling mechanisms are provided in SQL that return error information so that users or programmers will be able to perform corrective measures in enhancing the database system.

Final Words

Hope you have enjoyed this book and have got a lot of value from the information you have digested!

If you did enjoy it, I would truly appreciate if you could in return post an honest review on Amazon.

It certainly helps a lot and I would be dearly grateful.

Yours Truly,

Steve Gosling

www.ingramcontent.com/pod-product-compliance
Lightning Source LLC
La Vergne TN
LVHW022321060326
832902LV00020B/3596